"Many are sound asleep because they don't know about this gold mine of infinite intelligence and boundless love within themselves. What ever you want, you can draw forth."

- Joseph Murphy

This book is dedicated to all of you who are ready to be awakened.

Awaken The Divine

The Key to Power, Peace and Plenty

A Revision Of
"Three Magic Words"

Revised By:
Tricia Topping

U.S. Andersen   1917-1986

Contents

Introduction

Uell Stanley Andersen was a successful American self-help and short story author in the 1950's and 1960s. Most known for his book "Three Magic Words" a forerunner of the Law of Attraction Information.

When I read "Three Magic Words" I knew it held the key to unlock the secrets of the soul. The information that pours out of his book is filled with the guidance to have perfect health, freedom, wealth, love, oneness, and much more.

I myself have been a student of personal growth for many years and continue on my journey.

I have read piles of books, been to many spiritual and personal growth seminars. I have traveled near and far for the answers to life's mysteries.

Questions like, what am I? What caused me? Why am I here? And where am I going? It is said that when the student is ready the teacher will appear.

When I started reading "Three Magic Words" I knew right away U.S. Andersen was about to open many doors and answer many questions that I had.

Andersen's clear intentions are to help all individuals break free from the life they don't want to the life they desire and deserve.

The pages of this book feature the most powerful tools a person needs to be, do and have the life they've always dreamed. U.S. Andersen shows the way to oneness, fulfillment, wholeness, and freedom.

I have taken his book, broke it down and exposed the most important life transforming information people need to create the life of their dreams.

Each chapter title belongs to the author. I have carefully selected the teachings and phrases that will educate and empower anyone who reads them. I have also incorporated quotes from successful men and women who have applied these teachings and how they have achieved and guarded their successes.

If everyone owned a copy of "Three Magic Words" at a young age this world would be a very different place.

"When the mind is still, then the truth gets her chance to be heard in the purity of silence."   – Sri Aurobindo

In the pages of this book you will learn of the unlimited power that is yours. You will learn how you can turn this power to work for you, here on earth, to make your life majestic and overflowing with good.

This book is not a sect or a religion or a society. In its entirety it is a series of essays aimed at revealing to you your power over all things. You will learn that there is only one mover in all creation and that mover is thought.

You will learn that there is only one Creator and that Creator is Universal Subconscious Mind, or God. You will learn that this Creator creates for you exactly what you think, and you will be shown how you can control your thoughts, not only to obtain answers to your problems but to create in your experience exactly what you desire.

There is a power greater than you are, which you are a part of, which you can use to make your life great and full of abundance!

Chapter 1: The Lock

"If someone is going down the wrong road, he doesn't need motivation to speed him up. What he needs is education to turn him around."

– Jim Rohn

Somewhere there is a child being born. Somewhere, your spirit is inspired into form. And even now the lock takes shape. Mighty is the anvil that forges the lock, for it is the memory of the subconscious mind. Subconscious memory, forging the lock that bars the door to the infinite.

Negative thought patterns are the greatest bar to your discovery to yourself. They shape our lives until the time comes when we stop and ask ourselves, "Is this the life I really want?" When we grow into adulthood we search for the keys to unlock the door to freedom.

The only way you can become free to achieve success, happiness, and health is to arrive at truth – unlock the lock – discover the key!

THE PROMPTER-PAIN REJECTION

Growing up your conscious mind has experienced things like rejection, resentment, jealousy, fear, and the subconscious mind stores these memories. These memories are the prompters. Negative prompters have been the cause of hostility, insecurity, corruption, greed and hate. These prompters are the lock. They have been buried by the Conscious Mind, much as a forgetful dog might bury a bone, remembering not the place of burial nor even the fact of burial.

Negative prompters (memories) have thrown mankind out of tune with the infinite. They are the lock that bars the door to self–realization. People who are poverty-stricken will tell you that the last thing they want is to be in the situation that they are in. No matter what they do it ends up in a negative outcome. Why?

How many times have we heard, "There is never enough to go around," "Money is so hard to come by," "Money doesn't grow on trees," or "I will never be able to afford that." The subconscious mind will believe all of the above and a manifestation of lack will appear.

"You can't have a better tomorrow if you're thinking about yesterday."
                                            –Charles Kettering

There are people who desire love and companionship, who are very alone. There are prompters in this person that repels love such as, "I never do anything right," "no one cares about me," or "I'm not good enough." These prompters become your reality.

Who can rise to heights with a prompter that has them believing that they have no capability? The answer is no one. The good news is that you can remove all of these negative prompters yourself. Nothing is impossible to the mind of man, for conscious mind controls the subconscious mind and subconscious mind is all-powerful.

Every condition, circumstance, and manifestation of your life can be changed to suit your conscious desires. The Commandments are only two: Know that fear is your enemy and understand the lock.

Fear causes the lock, and the lock exists in the subconscious mind in the form of prompters, placed by the conscious mind. This starts the journey of undoing the lock:

You are pure spirit, cast into human mold as a manifestation of divine intelligence, existing this little while on Earth to help carry on the divine plan.

Being pure in spirit, you are a part of all the intelligence there is, and all the power and understanding of this intelligence are yours to draw upon.

There is only one intelligence, one mind in all creation, and everyone is a part of it. The Universal Subconscious Mind that flows through everyone knows no limitation or lack, and nothing is impossible to it.

Its great dominant characteristic is creativeness. Since it is all knowledge and all substance and all power, indeed the only thing it does is create. And it creates exactly what the mind of each individual person thinks into it.

We are discussing something that you use every day of your life, that you can't help but use because it is a part of you, in fact, is altogether the real you.

The Universal Mind knows no big or little, rich or poor, great or insignificant. It gives of itself according to need, and it creates according to desire. It is creating for you exactly what you are thinking into it.

"We think in secret and it comes to pass, environment is but our looking glass."

–James Allen

Simple Formula:

Thoughts plus conviction (firmly held belief) equals manifestation. There is manifested in your experience exactly that which you are convinced of. If our subconscious prompters believe success to be impossible, then our emotional thought is aimed at failure and failure will be the result.

So, what is the hardest thing to do for all of us? Wrapping our minds around the truth about what really is. That we are pure spirit and we are a part of all the intelligence that is. All the power and understanding is ours to draw upon. We can be, do and have everything we desire as long as we BELIEVE that we can. And the truth is...WE CAN!

REPETITION

We learned how to read, write, and even spell our own names through repetition. So repeating positive affirmations to oneself is a sure way to override those negative prompters.

First, however, we must be concerned with removing all the negative prompters from the subconscious mind and installing a group of positive prompters which will lead us in the path of attainment and happiness. Removing these negative prompters is not a hard task.

Since positive overrides negative, all that is necessary is for us to install in the subconscious a group of positive prompters. The existence of these will dissipate all negative prompters and allow the individual to expand to the full blossom of his or her power.

Affirmations like:
- It is natural to attract and give love because I am love.
- Abundance flows freely to me
- Every cell in my body dances with energy and health
- I am now ALLOWING (what ever you desire) to come into my life.

"It is repetition of affirmations that leads to belief. And once that belief becomes a deep conviction, things begin to happen."

– Claude M. Bristol

It took us time to install all of these negative prompters that stop us from having the life that we deserve. Now let's take some time to line up with truth and install positive prompters that will lead us to the life that we came here for.

CREATOR

Faith– Complete trust or confidence in someone or something.

Faith, the mover of mountains, the worker of miracles, is the conscious mind acting on the subconscious mind. We need to only concern ourselves with intuition (A thing that one knows or considers likely from instinctive feeling rather than conscious reasoning) and Faith, for by Faith we will overcome the lock, and through intuition we will contact the infinite.

Nothing is impossible to the human mind when the lock is removed. So why does it seem difficult for us to have the life we dream of? The answer is simple. Most of us were not brought up with teachings on power, peace, and plenty.

Most were taught that everything is hard to come by and everything is a struggle. None of that is true, but we see with our eyes day-to-day people doing and saying just that. And that became our entrapment.

"When a person really desires something, all the universe conspires to help that person realize his dream."

–Paulo Coelho

The entrapment is easily undone with daily affirmations that ring true to your heart. Saying things like, "I am a CEO of a big company and I make lots of money" could actually hurt you rather than help. After saying something like that you will check with reality and reality will tell you that's not true.

Saying affirmations like, "Being a leader comes natural to me," "Abundance flows freely into my life," and "I'm allowing great health" will send you down the river with ease and on your way to your desires in life.

There is no end to individual power through the right use of thought. Thought plus faith = Creation

JOURNEY TOWARDS GOD

Man is pure in spirit, in essence a part of God, in actuality a manifestation of the infinite. Negative prompters act as a bar to the door of the infinite, keeping us from full contact with the power of the great Universal Mind in which we live, move, and have our being.

It is possible that you will be unready to accept the complete realization of your own divine origin and power.

Yet inside you, a still small voice knows the truth, and no matter the strength of your rebellion away from your true self, the fact of your spiritual existence, the great I Am, will not be denied.

"There is nothing that I cannot be, do, or have, and I have a huge nonphysical staff that's ready to assist me."

–Abraham

Ester & Jerry Hicks

The understanding of this power within yourself will expand your life to new and exciting horizons and will embark you upon the greatest adventure ever known.

THE RESULT OF SELF KNOWINGNESS

The results of all self-knowingness is formed, and so your form, or body is the result of you knowing yourself, being aware of yourself. Your body is the embodiment of life, is an expression of life, for through your body your spirit expresses itself.

It matters not the form of your body, for it is perfect, as spirit within is perfect. It is a perfect instrument for the expression of your spirit, and only the misuse of spiritual law can cast from its perfection. For God is perfect, Spirit is perfect, and the body that expresses them must be perfect.

Your only job is to keep thinking right thoughts. Pure and positive thoughts create the power bond between you and God, The Creator, Higher Power, Universal Mind, what ever you feel fit to call it. Unhealthy thoughts like, I'm too old, too young, I'm not good enough, I'm too heavy, too skinny, or I've made too many mistakes, will break the bond between you and your power.

Negative thoughts have never served you up to this point and they never will. It's time for a shift.

"You deserve well-being, and well-being is making its way to you at all times. If you will relax and find a way to allow it – it will be in your experience."

–Abraham

Ester and Jerry Hicks

THE TRUTH LIES LOOKING INWARD

There is a great medium of mind and intelligence that is in and surrounds every human being. This intelligence is all-intelligence, God, an internal Creator, creating that which the mind of man thinks.

So great is the new found newly recognized power of thought, that groups around the world are aiming at the creation of peace through thought power. What else is this but prayer? Done correctly and with power it must succeed.

"What some call miracles are only the use of the law of mind in action. Change the idea of a thing, and you change the thing. It's that simple."

–Dr. Earnest Holmes

This great plastic creative medium, this Subconscious Mind, this mind of the universe in which there is all knowledge, all wisdom, and all power, is ours to use every day that we live. We are using it now. We can't help but use it. More often than not we are using it in such a manner as to create unhappy circumstance and situations, delaying if not forbidding the realization of our own God-given divinity.

It is important for you to understand that you are a part of the Great Intelligence. The limitations you impose on yourself must dissipate. You can draw upon the infinite for those divine powers that are yours.

To understand ourselves better we have to realize we are not a name, a job title, not our cars we drive, nor our bank accounts. There is not another you and there never has been.

CREATIVENESS

We compare ourselves too much to a point where most of us feel discouraged. The essence of mankind is not competition. It is creativeness. If we are constantly comparing ourselves we will never take the time to create ourselves, and we can become lost in a battle that is unforgiving.

Competition attempts to be like. Creativeness attempts to be unlike. Conformity and competition are detrimental to the spirit. Creativeness and non-conformity are an expansion to the spirit.

By concentrating on our goals and desires, we will end up with what we really want and not what we think we should have. Competition puts a strain on people and makes us feel "we have to" instead of feeling like we want to.

If we are in a creative state of mind, that gives us the freedom to come up with ideas from our hearts and not from what we would consider a competitor.

ENLIGHTENMENT

Your security in life depends entirely on your recognition of your divine nature. Only that great unity – your own association with the infinite, your manifestation of the Universal Mind of God will provide you with such security as you have ever dreamed, will cast into proper perspective every aspect of your life, will unloose in you such a flood of creative energy as to fill your life to brimming success, accomplishment and good health.

Only diligent daily application of these truths will finally dissipate all doubt. Faith is the great mover, the father of all creation. The Universal Mind is responsive to thought. It creates what is projected into it. Study and experiment with your own Divine nature. Discover for yourself the great source of power and wisdom that exists within you.

DON'T ARGUE WITH YOURSELF

Subsequent chapters will cover such subjects as illusion, mind, form, faith, intuition, love, success, health, attraction and immortality. This book will show how they are all products of the vast power of the Universal Subconscious mind.

"Believe it can be done. When you believe something can be done, really believe, your mind will find the ways to do it. Believing a solution paves the way to solution."

–Dr. David Schwartz

Enlightenment however, is not going to be as simple as just reading the chapters. You must devote at least 10 minutes a day to the practice of what you have learned, for only with this cooperation and effort can the rewards of self-realization be achieved.

Project your thoughts into the creative Subconscious Mind, so they can manifest into actuality. Of course if you spend 10 minutes each day saying positive things and the other 23 hours and 50 minutes saying negative things, the negative will result.

Therefore, commit the positive thoughts to memory or carry them on paper with you. Throughout the day, when circumstances appear to be negative, simply bring the positive thoughts to your mind and say them over and over to yourself.

The simple saying of the words will immediately restore your peace and confidence. When you feel calm and peaceful, you will know that you are in contact with the Universal Mind. Then and only then, speak the positive affirmations aloud. But don't simply speak them. Understand them, FEEL them, project them. They will manifest for you in actuality.

The Universal Mind knows the answers to all of your problems, and they are speeding their way to you.

CHAPTER 2: ILLUSION

In chapter two you will begin to understand that God is truth, and evil (bad conduct or causing harm) is error. We control our very circumstances as we sift through life with our own perception of things. Andersen teaches us that what we believe, good or evil, will inevitably develop in our experience, and that evil is only illusion.

EVIL-THE GREAT ILLUSION

The painful idea of hell as a place of punishment for sin is man's own morbid idea. Evil is man's own morbid idea. Disease and suffering are man's own morbid ideas. God does not know of the existence of these things. Since he created man free, he has left it up to man to conceive their own situations.

If God is a God of love he did not create evil. As far as man's earthly life is concerned, if you believe in evil, you experience evil.

It has to be understood that each human being is a living embodiment of God and that God is in you and around you. Each human being creates through thought. It can be proven that disease and suffering and evil of every kind are created by man and man alone.

The subconscious mind is like a garden, and like the garden of earth that knows only to cause things to grow, the garden of the subconscious mind knows only to create reality from the seed of thought. Whether this thought is moral or immoral has nothing to do with the unstoppable process involved. For the seed having been planted must grow, and grow it will, into physical fact, unless the seed itself is uprooted and another planted in its place.

FREEDOM-THE ESSENCE OF MANKIND

Don't forget for an instance of a day in your life that you are free. That freedom is the most miraculous part of your existence. God allowed you to create what you will. He endowed you with the instinct of survival and progress so that when you create something contrary to your own good, the lesson should keep you from creating it again.

God made man only to create through thoughts. Beyond that, each person chooses their own road.

MORALITY AND SPIRITUAL LAW

Success isn't the result of hard work, it is the result of right thinking. Put the seed of failure, disease, loneliness, or unhappiness in the Subconscious Mind and it will develop them for you. Evil, the tragic illusion.

Thought into the great creative Universal Subconscious Mind plus faith can equal only one thing, and this thing is physical reality. It matters not whether the thought is good or evil, if the faith is there it will manifest, for that is law. Thoughts plus faith creates.

SEE NO EVIL

Believe you will succeed and you will.
Believe you will fail and you will.
Believe you will be well and you will be.
Believe you will be sick and you will be.
Believe you are unloved and you are.
Believe you are beautiful and you are.

MANKIND'S STRUGGLE TOWARD TRUTH

We must see evil as it really is, simply illusion, simply a pain response, a wrong road taken, an experiment toward truth, but always an illusion. We are responsible for our thoughts and our beliefs. All else is the working of the great creative Universal Mind.

God sends his rain on the just and the unjust alike. For evil falls on the righteous and the unrighteous, but it cannot visit them who sees and is convinced of nothing but good.

TRUTH AND ERROR

Good is truth. Evil is error. If we know that evil proceeds from thought, just as good proceeds from thought, we can establish an eternal watch on our minds to guide our thoughts in the paths of good and progress.

For even the ultimate is not impossible of attainment this very moment if we have the faith and the imagination. Since good is truth and evil is error, it is then apparent that evil is illusion.

Evil is a wrong road, a mistake, a pain experience, simply a search on the road toward truth. Evil dissipates with complete ease. It is replaced by good with almost miraculous speed. Truth does not lightly yield to error, while error has few defenses against the light of truth.

Since truth is good and error is evil, the knowing of good forbids the choice of evil. There is no doubt that mankind stands at the threshold of spiritual freedom this very day. It is not only needed and desired, it is demanded by each person who lives, that we gain access to the laws that govern our life so that we may use them for our own benefit and the benefit of humanity as a whole.

As a human being, you will make mistakes in arriving at truth. Do not allow regret to become a prompter. Be joyful that error has disclosed truth.

Many of us today carry around a pile of remorse, regret, and shame. These feelings we carry will only pave the road to an unfulfilling lifestyle. Remember: the mistakes we make are what brings us closer to the life we desire.

When we do something that causes pain to ourselves or another, that pain is an indicator that we need to think about healthier choices.

"By our stumbling the world is perfected. Do not belong to the past dawns but to the noons of the future."

–Sri Aurobindo

"It's okay to make mistakes. Mistakes are our friends. They help us grow. Actually it is impossible to make a mistake in real terms, since everything that we call a "mistake" actually brings us benefit."

– Neale Donald Walsch

The tragic picture of the person dragging through life, chastising themselves of every mistake is the source and the cause of every negative prompter of the subconscious mind. To err is human, and every error in your life is for the purpose of revealing truth to you. Mistakes reveal to you a better path to take. They are not to stultify your Divinity in shame and remorse and fear.

You cannot live and not make mistakes. But this you can do. You can suffer the consequence of each mistake only once and learn from it. Let us not be afraid of making a mistake or of suffering the consequences if the mistake is made. Find a person who has suffered a score of defeats and you will find a great soul.

"To grow, you must be willing to let your present and future be totally unlike your past. Your history is NOT your destiny."

– Alan Cohen

DARE TO BE CONVINCED

If you make a mistake, there is no one and nothing that will hold you to account except the law of cause and effect, a strictly impersonal operating law. Once the consequence of that error has come upon you, you need have no fear that any others will be visited…. Unless you create them yourself!

If you carry from some error remorse and chastisement, these feelings must act on the subconscious mind to create themselves in reality.

MAN MAKES CIRCUMSTANCE

Now it must be thoroughly understood that we are not denying the existence of evil. We are simply denying the reality of it, naming it illusion as it surely is.

No great man or woman has ever lived who has not risen above circumstance, literally denying the reality of lack, limitation, illness, poverty, and inferiority. If you allow yourself to become a product of circumstance, then each encounter you make with evil will convince you of the reality of it, and it will be created in your experience.

Don't think for a single minute that circumstance makes man. Man makes circumstance. Through the great Law of Attraction, all things come to you who believes in them. Every circumstance of your life inevitably has been attracted to you by your own beliefs.

You are literally a product of your own thoughts. You are what you think, only that and nothing more. The individual who habitually maintains a mental attitude of faith and expectancy of the best is bound to succeed and advance in life.

The individual who is depressed, morbid, and despondent attracts failure all along the line. Fear is truly a lack of faith in divine supply. Make a choice now! Begin to think constructively and harmoniously.

"To think is to speak. Your thought is your word."

– Joseph Murphy

THE POWER OF THE WORD

Today you may be walking around with a subconscious full of prompters that would have you be sick, poor, lonely, and unsuccessful. You must control these prompters or they will control you.

You must by conscious meditation on the spiritual laws of the universe, install in the subconscious a conditioned response for good, which will automatically displace all negative prompters.

You must do this or there is not the slightest possibility of the full and good life. The power of word or thought is such that nothing will stand against it as long as it is spoken with conviction.

"Happiness doesn't depend on who you are or what you have. It depends solely on what you think."

– Dale Carnegie

ACCEPT DON'T WILL

You cannot by yourself do the slightest bit of creating. The power into which you project your thoughts is the only creative force there is, and it builds and constructs all form and circumstance, but it does this according to how you think.

Now it is absolutely impossible for you to make this power do anything. You cannot by sheer force of will bend this power to suit your needs. You are not greater than God. You cannot either stop or start this power in its creating, for it is greater than you are and it moves according to law.

You cannot say "I'm going to make money" with all the determination and ferociousness you can muster and expect that you are creating in your experience anything other than belligerence and opposition.

You've got to allow, not demand. You cannot will anything. This simply means that you recognize that it is not you who does the creating. It is a power greater than you are. This power creates what you believe and manifests for you what you are allowing.

Be sure you understand this. All of your will for money will avail you nothing, for that is the wrong use of spiritual law. Money will be created in your experience only if you realize and know that there is an abundance all about you and you except it.

In other words, you don't demand money. You don't force money because of the feeling that there is not enough to go around, and you don't have enough of it. You allow money. There is a great abundance of it about you, and you know that. Therein lies the true use of spiritual law.

Expect and accept. Know and experience. Be positive and thankful. For the great laws of attraction and creation are laws of attunement and never make known their secrets to those who batter at the door with force. Know and except. Those are the secrets of all prayer and meditation.

"It's a funny thing about life. If you refuse to accept anything but the best, you very often get it.

– W Somerset Maugham

GUIDANCE THROUGH ATTUNEMENT

When you have completely accepted the power greater than you are, when you know it will create in your experience that which you believe, you will also find that it also will provide you with answers to your problems.

You must do this by letting go of your problem. Forget the problem altogether. One morning while you are going about your daily tasks you will find the answer. It will strike your consciousness with such impact as to remove all doubt but what is truth. The answer will be crystal clear, of such simplicity that you will be amazed that it never occurred to you before.

This is guidance. It is not achieved by any effort or will. It is achieved by confidence in the power greater than you are. It is achieved by complete acceptance of the power greater than you are.

If you are able to effect this complete attunement every minute of every day, there can be little doubt but what pain, lack, limitation and disease will never more exist in your experience.

If you say to yourself, "I know I am working along the paths of success" and go the rest of the day complaining about every obstacle you meet, you may wind up expecting that success should be yours, but it won't be.

Your faith must be with you fifty-one percent of the time before it will manifest in your experience. But a manifestation will come, one way or another, according to the strongest thought.

No human being can assume the responsibility for a single thing other than their own thinking, the Universal Subconscious Mind does all the creating.

Guidance and inspiration in the paths of truth and achievement can be yours through faith and reliance in the power greater than you are.

You are now experimenting with the greatest force in nature. We caution you not to become so wrapped up in it that you forget your daily life. As for being a human being your goal must be to achieve a perfect balance between conscious and subconscious mind.

Ordinary people we meet each day scarcely use the subconscious mind at all, and their lives are directed and controlled entirely by circumstance. Men and women of genius are those in whom there is perfect balance between the subconscious and conscious mind.

Cast aside all doubt and effort and strain. You don't have to make anything. It is already made. You only want to use it correctly. Except! Believe! Know! Relax! The universe will provide you with all you desire.

"Remember, all of the answers you need are inside of you; you only have to become quiet enough to hear them."

– Debbie Ford

"What ever you're thinking about is like planning a future event. What you're worrying about, you are planning. When you're appreciating, you are planning… What are you planning?"

–Abraham

Ester and Jerry Hicks

"I have learned over the years that when one's mind is made up, this diminishes fear; knowing what must be done does away with fear."

– Rosa Parks

Chapter 3: Mind

Chapter three teaches us the truth about mind. Andersen brings us to the understanding of "self" and in detail explains the difference between the conscious and subconscious mind. You will be taught the tools you will need to make anything a possibility in your life.

Chapter three is a true gold mine for the person that seeks mastery over one's self and unfailing success. For you cannot fail when you realize the power that all along has been in your possession.

"We are shaped by our thoughts; we become what we think. When the mind is pure, joy follows like a shadow that never leaves."

–Buddha

THE MYSTERY OF MIND

We give our approval to techniques which trace out brain convulsions and nerve networks and tell us of the storage compartments of memory, the pulpy mass that gives rise to imagination, the spinal network of conditioned responses.

These, we say are mind – these arrangements of matter which we generally investigate in a deceased person or in partially inanimate ones. Yet how far from the truth this is!

The impact and mystery of self-consciousness, the personal "I am," has never yielded its secrets to the surgeon's knife or the biologists probing. To objectively state that the body has a nerve center called the brain does not bring man one step closer to an understanding of his own self-existence.

In this chapter we shall turn from such half-truths into a world of personal consciousness, dealing with mind as divorced from the material, as pure thought and conception, as existing on the spiritual plane of cause and effect. In this manner we shall arrive at unity, the point where all things are one and thought is the only mover, the creator of everything.

"The reason why the world lacks unity, and lies broken, is because man is disunited with himself."

– Ralph Waldo Emerson

"Look out into the universe and contemplate the glory of God. Observe the stars, millions of them, twinkling in the night sky, all with a message of unity, part of the very nature of God."

– Sai Baba

THE INSTRUMENT OF SURVIVAL

The conscious mind of ours exists at the level of the five senses and is quite logically a product of hearing, seeing, smelling, feeling and tasting. Its pursuit is to satisfy each of these five senses with sensations which provide pleasure instead of pain.

The conscious mind therefore is a pleasure-pain distinguisher, and its compartments of memory, reason, and imagination are but names given to its total instinct to find pleasure and avoid pain.

All conscious organisms are endowed with the life urge to survive, and this life urge manifests itself in each as a conscious intelligence, best adapted to cope with its surroundings. This survival instinct must necessarily be based on a pleasure-pain principal, for pleasure is an assurance of survival while pain is a warning of destruction.

The experience of pain brings forth the desire to avoid pain, and the desire to avoid pain brings forth an image to escape it. This image is projected into the creative Universal Mind which manifests new form and new conscious intelligence to this life that seeks to cope with its surroundings.

FUNCTIONS OF THE CONSCIOUS MIND

The conscious mind is a recording, analyzing, and a selected instrument for sensation. As an instrument of sensation, the conscious mind is limited, a thing of this world, a structural part of a working organism without use or purpose once that organism has ceased to be.

Now, of itself the conscious mind has no memory. In other words, it does not contain a store house in which is laid up all experience and sensation. The faculty of memory as applied to the conscious mind is simply its ability to recall certain experiences and conclusions which have been recorded in the subconscious mind.

The memory of the subconscious mind is perfect. Every thought of the conscious mind has been recorded in the subconscious as well as every sensory perception of the individual. The great mass of this material is forever lost to the recall of the conscious mind, for it can only be recalled when it has previously been filed away with instructions to the subconscious mind to release it for recall.

BENEATH THE LEVEL OF CONSCIOUSNESS

It can be seen that subconscious memory contains a vast store of material - premises, conclusions, and perceptions - that exist without the knowledge of the conscious mind.

This vast store of knowledge beneath the level of consciousness affords a great portion of the existing power in each individual person, for could you this moment recall all this knowledge perfectly, your efficiency and wisdom as an individual would be increased a thousand-fold.

These memories simply exist, a huge amount of experience and knowledge lying dormant. But there lies in the subconscious mind convictions which have been filed away by the conscious mind with the express order never to be available for recall - the prompters.

Here in these pain rejections, these conclusions which the conscious mind could not bear to tolerate, these images of conviction which have been buried from sight, we find our illusionary devil truly at work.

For the nature of the Universal Intelligence is that it responds to conviction; and the prompters move the subconscious mind to those very things which the individual fears.

In order to truly grasp the significance of the relationship between man and the Universal Mind, we must start at the beginning. The conscious mind is but a small part of a gigantic whole. Power and wisdom are within reach of every intelligent person.

MASS AND ENERGY ARE ONE

Based on pure scientific research, the only possible conclusion is that there is only one substance from which everything physical is made. There is only one substance from which all energy is made and this energy or substance, is infinite in time and space. It has no beginning and no end and it is everywhere at all times, and all of it is anywhere at any time.

The astounding discovery of science, that there is no such thing as a solid mass, has revised the thinking of the entire world. This may prove to be a substantial dose to digest, but if you are going to throw off the shackles of limited thinking, you must strive to free yourself from conceptions of form, mass, space, and time as ultimate reality.

You must say to yourself that you know that the physical world as you see it could not possibly answer the question of your own existence, so the answer must be elsewhere. You must reach into the furthermost recesses of your mind, for the answer is there and only there and never in the physical world around you.

"Seeing is not always believing."

–Martin Luther King Jr.

"Faith consists in believing when it is beyond the power of reason to believe." – Voltaire

We now know that matter and energy are one, that there is only one substance or energy or intelligence in all things. Since in its pure form, we can recognize this energy as nothing but invisible power, unintelligible to our five senses, there is not the slightest valid reason to assume that it is anything else than constant and never changing its basic nature.

It always has been and always will be; in other words, that it is limitless. Everything is basically one thing, infinite. We are all one... Only egos, beliefs, and fears separate us.

"Three things cannot be hidden; the sun, the moon, and the truth."   – Buddha

INFINITY AND GOD

Infinity is a difficult word since words are attempts to convey thoughts, the word infinity has come to cover a multitude of so-called unknowables. Infinity is the word science has substituted for God. This is not to assign to science in irreverent attitude, for scientists as a group of men and women are the most reverent in creation.

Scientists simply cannot work with the unknowable, and religion says that God cannot be known. Infinity, says science, is that oneness behind all creation that can be known. But, of course, we are not talking about two different things at all.

God is one; infinity is one. God is everywhere; Infinity is everywhere. God is an everlasting now; Infinity is an everlasting now. God knows everything. Infinity contains everything.

All the thinking efforts of man are but different roads which lead to one common destination:
Infinity or God, which ever you will.

Infinity or God is all form and yet is but one form. Infinite, eternal, only one, and never changing, that to which all things are known in which every physical object has its being – this is God, and all of God is in us this moment, right now, and all the moments to come.

THE GRAND CONCEPTION

If we have lost you now, it is only because your conception of the final reality of the physical world is so strong that for the moment it will not dissolve before your efforts to free your mind.

If you are wondering whether this is dream or substance, fact or fiction, simply keep your faith. Be assured of this: all the mystery and complexity will disappear. As you continue to study and meditate you will one day read again the portions of this book which seemed complex and will be amazed at how fundamental and simple they seem to you.

You are gathering from each chapter far more than you know, coming closer to an understanding of your true self, breaking down the limited walls in your thinking, undergoing an expansion in power and conception that you may as yet be unaware of.

So let's stand for the moment on the conclusion that there is but one power behind the entire universe which is everywhere at all times and is the substance from which all things are made.

This infinite intelligence spreads through all life-all vegetable and animal life and even every lifeless looking object of our world. This infinite intelligence is the only mind there is; we are all using it, we can't help but use it, for it is one and everywhere, and is the stuff from which all things are made. One mind which is everywhere and everything. This is the Subconscious Mind.

EXPOSING THE SUBCONSCIOUS

The Subconscious Mind does not by itself make choices, indulge in arguments, create theories, search for answers, wonder at possibilities. It only accepts and acts. Once it is given a suggestion by the conscious mind, it immediately sets to work to make that suggestion truth, for it accepts that suggestion completely.

What few people have suspected over the years is that the Subconscious Mind not only accepts suggestion as truth, but it has the capacity to make literal truth out of each suggestion!

The Subconscious Mind is everything, contains everything, and therefore can do anything. All it needs is the suggestion. All matter, all substance, all knowledge exists within it, and it rearranges them according to suggestion.

"After 14 years practical experience with suggestive therapeutics in the treatment of patients, I have no hesitation in saying that the most important study connected with the art of healing is the study of auto-suggestion; but auto-suggestion plays such a vital part in our daily lives, in the forming of character and in our successes and our failures, that it should be studied and understood by everyone in every walk of life."

–Herbert A Parkyn

Author of -"Autosuggestion-
"What It Is And How To Use It For Health Happiness And Success."

It is only within the last few years that we have thoroughly recognized the existence of one of the greatest forces in nature: Auto-Suggestion

Auto-suggestion:
Self -impression- An impression made on one's self, or an idea arising within one's own mind.

Nothing is impossible to the subconscious mind and it operates entirely by suggestion. Here at last we see pure God–power, the Infinite, the mighty Subconscious Mind at work; for it creates according to the pure word or thought and is the single power in all creation.

"What we can or cannot do, what we consider possible or impossible, is rarely a function of our true capability. It is more likely a function of our beliefs about who we are."
– Tony Robbins

This Subconscious Mind belongs to no person alone, for in it and through it, all things live and have their beings. Since it is limitless, it is indivisible and therefore not able to be changed, and all likeness is tied together by an invisible but powerful bond.

ALL KNOWING MIND

"My full effort is to get myself out of the way and let something take over. When something takes over, the story gets written in jig time and is far superior to anything I alone could do. Naturally, I'd rather have something do it. Happily, something usually does."

– Adela Rogers

Every great artist and engineer, physicist, chemist, and astronomer, all who seek after creation and answers, must inevitably have some contact with the Universal Subconscious Mind. This contact comes when they get themselves out of the way and let the only mind in all creation provide them with the answers.

The Subconscious Mind reasons deductively. It cannot reason inductively because it already knows all spiritual law. It seeks only to determine circumstance from its complete knowledge of the law, therefore has in its possession the full knowledge of all governing law. This is indisputable proof that it is the infinite substance, God in man, the ultimate or absolute of all creation. It is obvious that the individual's complete use of this mind will provide them with all the power of creation.

This is your life. You will live it to its fullest possibilities only when you are able to consciously exercise the great power that belongs to you. You are living this life now, and live you must. The only answer is to arrive at understanding of the mighty forces of which you are a part of this minute and of which you are a part forevermore.

MEDITATION AFFIRMS SUGGESTION

Our primary tool in attaining all of our desires is the use of meditation. In meditation we are simply affirming certain suggestions to the Subconscious Mind. We are simply repeating and affirming certain thoughts with faith and conviction so that they will be acted upon by the Infinite Intelligence.

Only by attaining control and understanding of your own power will you truly be a master of your own life. Doctors and psychiatrists will play an important role in human welfare for many years to come. But the day will arrive when mankind understands that all physical circumstance originates on the plane of thought, and that day each person will stand guard against all disease and all emotional suffering, and suffering will disappear from our world.

We may call upon the power of all creation simply through thought and conviction. Nothing is impossible to man, for the Intelligence in which we live gives us anything we can visualize and have faith in. So let us not allow our conscious minds to trick us into believing that the physical world is the ultimate reality.

Let us go through our days following the dictates of the conscious mind in the physical world, for this pain–pleasure discerner of ours is a finely made machine for coping with the physical. But let us constantly reach outward for the infinite intelligence that is ours.

let us know that all form in circumstances must first originate on the plane of thought, that the first cause of all creation is simply thought through conviction. Let us know that we can contact the Universal Mind for all of our problems. That we can create all of our own circumstances by giving birth to them in our own minds.

Nothing in all the universe, can stop thoughts from becoming real in our experience for that is the law of life and of living.

FIRST CAUSE IS MENTAL

You are immortal; not your body, not your conscious mind, but the real you, the part of you which exist forever in the Universal Subconscious Mind. You always have been; you always will be. You are inseparably one with everything that is. Each human being in this world, all form, all objects. One, just one, and everything answers through faith.

All things and all circumstances must first be created on the mental plane. When such creation is clear-cut and born of faith in conviction, nothing can stop this image from becoming real. Once this image has come into your mind and you have accepted it, you have done all that is necessary for you to do. All the process of creation, time, place, and circumstance must be left in the hands of the All–Knowing Subconscious Mind.

The physical circumstance you desire may come from the direction you expect or it may come in such a way and such a manner as you have never dreamed. Don't strain or urge or become impatient. Simply have faith and let go. Remember, whatever you observe closely Can cause you to entertain an element of doubt.

You have nothing to do but create the mental image with complete faith, and with that simple act the process is completely done. Be assured that the image will become real in your physical world, for you are dealing with law and law alone.

Meditation is the tool with which we work. It is our way of giving suggestion to the subconscious mind. You must not fail to engage in your meditation period daily. Only through the constant use of this great tool can you achieve control over your circumstance and your destiny.

You will succeed, for you cannot fail. You are dealing with life force. You are life force. Power through self-realization is the destiny of man.

CHAPTER 4:   FORM

"The universe hums like a great harp string
Resounding a mighty cord
Answering each thought by returning a thing
In the place where all things stored."

In this chapter Andersen teaches on the design and flow of all energy, the stuff from which all things are made. If we study the beginning of all things and how all things are created then this knowledge alone allows us to understand how thought calls form into all existence. Form is no more than a part of the very Intelligence that each of us lives in. Andersen explains that when we can comprehend and accept the fact of oneness, the purpose of life is no longer unknown.

"Be faithful to that which exists in yourself"

–Andr'e Gide

THE UNIVERSE IS LAW

Our premise is that thought makes things; and in order to provide evidence to such a transcendent truth, we must turn to the beginning of all form. What is the basic substance that spreads through all space and time?

If we take apart a substance and discover atoms, and take apart the atom and unleash energy, we must eventually say the basic thing behind all form in all creation is energy.

Energy becomes apparent only in matter or movement, and always such a matter or movement attains an intelligent existence or moves in an intelligent direction. The design and flow of all energy is such as to leave no doubt that basic and eternal in the universe are everlasting and unchanging laws of action which alone account for the accumulation of substance into form.

Indeed, lacking a specific viewpoint or a scale of relativity, the solar system and the atom are identical, as they assuredly must be in the Universal Subconscious Mind.

A LIVING UNIVERSE

This Universal Subconscious Mind, this energy, then is the stuff from which all things are made. In its pure form it is represented only by intelligent movement or by a word which seems much more clear to describe it: Law. In the smallest scale we know is represented by the atom; on the largest scale we know is represented by the solar system.

Law is one of life and movement and energy which by its own nature gathers itself into units of smaller frequency in a vibrating universe. Vibration is intelligence alone and the force it exerts is of intelligence.

The vibrations in pure Universal Intelligence are established on many different frequencies and all vibrations of a frequency are attracted together to form a unit.

This unit, the center of corresponding vibrations, we know as an atom, or as the Solar System, the first sign of visible form, called into existence by the very nature of infinite law acting within and upon itself.

The formed atoms also sets up a vibration and seeks out other atoms of a corresponding vibration, and in this coming together of units vibrating on the same frequency there is formed matter as we know it in our physical world.

This matter is formed from intelligence, and more important intelligence is in matter; in fact, intelligence must be conscious, it is an indisputable fact that we are surrounded by a living universe, that there is consciousness in all things.

THE CONSCIOUSNESS OF THE ATOM

Now you must bear with this very necessary discussion of the beginning of things in the nature of substance, for we are out to show that thought calls form into existence, and that form is no more than a part of the very intelligence that each of us lives in.

The atom, the building block of the universe, is a center force, and the atom is conscious! Working in accordance with law of universal intelligence the atom seeks out other atoms which vibrate at a similar rate. The coming together of such atoms forms that which we designate as inanimate matter; water, earth, air, and minerals.

EXPANDING CONSCIOUSNESS

The entire universe is alive. There is nothing dead, nothing is lifeless. This is the basic truth of all creation. All is living and all is intelligence and all is conscious.

The great motivating force of all life is its attempt to expand its consciousness. In other words, it seeks to know itself. Though we can safely attribute consciousness and intelligence to the atom, there remains not the slightest possibility that the atom is self-conscious. In fact, all evidence points to the consciousness of the atom being of the lowest possible order.

It chooses, but its choices are within the rigid scope of operating law. When a certain number of atoms begin vibrating together on a certain frequency, let us say a rock, there is created in the rock a kind of consciousness which is on an infinitely lower scale than that of the atom.

There can be no doubt that there is a certain consciousness in the rock, for a group of conscious units must form a group of consciousness. It consists of conscious intelligence and must then have some consciousness of its own.

From the rock and sand, earth, water, and air to the formation of the pain-pleasure responsive amoeba, a thing grows and feeds and reproduces itself. What a gigantic step is this! Expanding consciousness! Only that and nothing more.

First, we have energy moving according to law, congregating into centers of force by its own nature, setting up polarization. These centers of force or atoms, have lives of their own and are conscious.

The nature of these little lives is to congregate with others vibrating on the same frequency, and this matter is called into existence which is basically not matter at all, but merely units of intelligent energy.

Secondly, we have all form consisting of many individual lives, building up to a conscious whole, and building up to a conscious entity which attempts to work out its own purpose.

From these two conclusions we go on to a third: The form which results from the union of many individual lives or consciousness is the result of the consciousness of the whole. In other words, the form of the rock is the result of the consciousness of the rock. The form of the amoeba is a result of the consciousness of the amoeba. The form of the human is the result of the consciousness of the human being.

LIFE SEEKS TO KNOW ITSELF

The entire universe is caught up in a mighty work of expanding consciousness because it is the nature of Universal Intelligence to seek to know itself. God only knows himself as a thing. Space as we know it, or the Universal Subconscious Mind as we know it cannot possibly have any limits or boundaries.

How is it possible for something which has no boundaries to ever know itself? In order to know itself it must be able to say, "I am this." In order for it to say, "I am this" it must become something with boundaries, something with limits, a thing.

That is exactly what the Universal Subconscious Mind is doing. It is becoming things. It is seeking an expanded version of itself. And that part of it which has achieved the greatest self-consciousness which we are able to observe is the human being.

What is evolution? It is life expanding to a conscious oneness with God. As time progresses and our consciousness expands, we are growing closer and closer to this attainment. Indeed, this is the clue to the mystery of life and the evolution and the destiny of man.

The destiny of mankind is that our consciousness will expand to the point where we are one with all creation. Our consciousness will be the consciousness of God.

COSMIC AWARENESS

It can be seen that the purpose of life is the attainment of knowledge, the expansion of consciousness, a constant reaching upward and inward towards oneness with God. Thought makes form. Thought makes things.

For we are all one in reality, and our separateness is nothing but a necessary illusion in the plan by which Universal Mind seeks to know itself by becoming a thing. Perception of the indwelling presence is often difficult to come by.

And as the years gradually enlarged my consciousness, there came a day when I too looked on all things and saw God. On that day my faith, weak in questioning as it might have been, was tempered by this steel of knowledge.

"Quantum physics reveals a basic oneness of the universe"

– Erwin Schrodinger

"It is difficult to believe in yourself because the idea of self is an artificial construction. You are, in fact part of the glorious oneness of the universe. Everything beautiful in the world is within you."

– Russell Brand

"The first place, which is the most important, is that which comes within the souls of people when they realize their relationship, their oneness with the universe and all its powers, and when they realize that at the center of the universe dwells the Great Spirit, and that this center is really everywhere, it is within each of us."

– Black Elk

"So powerful is the light of unity that it can illuminate the whole world."   – Baha'u'llah

"The goal of the creator is for each entity to make a conscious choice to again seek oneness, out of our own free will – not because anyone forced us to. Perhaps the most basic realization to make is that we live in a loving universe. If we are all one being, then it is foolish for us to hate anyone, as we are only hating ourselves."

                                                        – David Wilcock

"The fundamental delusion of humanity is to suppose that I am here and you are out there."

                                                        – Yasutani Roshi

"Man must begin in the unitary principle of man–knowing that they are not separate men or separate individuals, but that the whole man idea is one. He must know that all mankind is connected with every other part of mankind, all geared together by the one omnipresent light of God which centers all as ONE and motivates all as ONE. Until man knows that separation from God is impossible, even for one second, he does not begin to have knowledge."

–Walter Russell

GROWING INTO UNDERSTANDING

You first have to understand what mind is. We must be sure your consciousness has been expanded to the point where you recognize that conception and thought are the alpha and omega of all existence. Patience is the virtue you can best exercise now and thoughtfulness with the conceptions you are now entertaining and evolving.

REALITY VERSES DELUSION

We attach our fleeting securities to the forms around us, vainly trying to build up a sense of permanence in a constantly changing material world, forgetting the mystery of all births and the inevitability of our deaths as we put our main goal on the accumulation of wealth and goods.

Yet all form is made of the same basic substance as ourselves, pure and eternal Intelligence; the Universal Subconscious Mind; and that mind, all it contains lies within each of us. Form is no more than conception, form is no more than an idea.

Form always involves consciousness and it is entirely representative of thought. In its pure essence, form is constructed of exactly the same material from which a thought is constructed.

DUAL MIND

Our education and inhibition have been such as to teach us that thought has evolved in our attempt to deal with things, while the truth is that things are no more than images that represent our thoughts.

All truths exist within you and never in the world about you. Those who study the world study effects. Those who study their own mind study the cause and the source of things as they really are.

A QUESTIONING GOD

Beneath the illusion of separateness there lies a great unity of all things, a unity in which space and time and individual form are all combined into one, an underlying infinite spirit or in intelligence, the Universal Subconscious Mind.

Here it is reasonable to ask: if this is so, what is the purpose of the illusion of separateness. What is the purpose of individual lives and individual things? And the only reasonable answer at which it is possible to arrive is that the Universal Subconscious Mind is seeking to know itself by becoming things, that, in effect, it cannot know itself as infinity.

The only possible conclusion is that there is only one purpose behind evolving life and that purpose is an expanding consciousness. God seeks to know himself by becoming a thing.

THE UNIQUENESS OF YOU

The universe is engaged in making numbers of unlike things from a basic oneness. By its very nature it cannot make two things which are completely identical. If two conceptions are completely alike, there is only one conception that would produce only one thing.

One of the biggest barriers in the explanation of the unity of life is that a person will say, "If true mind is universal and in all things, why am I me and not someone else or even everyone else?" And the only answer which is possible to give is that you are someone else and even everyone else basically.

The difference you perceive between yourself and others is simply the difference between the thoughts you have had, for each person is only what they think.

You are what you are only because of what you have thought. Because this thought is different from any person who has ever lived, you are a unique thing in the universe.

Most of your thinking is prompted by the sensations that come to you through your five senses. Since these belong to your body exclusively, you are constantly building up experience and thoughts that keep you locked away from oneness with the Universal Subconscious Mind.

THE KINGDOM OF GOD IS WITHIN

We must understand that all form and matter represent only the same intelligence that is in us. We must recognize that all Intelligence is ours to draw upon and to understand and use. We must know that thought makes form, thought makes things, and thought makes us what we are.

We must know that our separateness is only of evolving consciousness, that basically there is complete spiritual unity of all life. We must strive constantly to expand our consciousness by identifying ourselves with everything and everyone about us.

We must search in our quiet hours for contact with the Universal Subconscious Mind, where all information and all thought have been without a doubt impressed, which can guide us unerringly along the paths of attainment and knowledge.

We must understand the invincible power of thought, how it makes us what we are, how it creates form and brings circumstance, how it underlies and moves the universe. We must guard ourselves from being exposed to negative thinking; we must refuse to accept negative circumstance.

We must, in our complete and positive expansion, and our soaring knowledge of the mighty work of the mind, teach our children to control their thinking. Teach our neighbors to control their thinking. Teach a suffering mankind that the way out of each dilemma lies in the vehicle of its own thought. The Kingdom of God is within every one of us.

MIND IS GREATER THAN ALL

Nothing is impossible to the intelligence that knows all things, the Universal Subconscious Mind. All of this guidance and power are available to you. When you have fully realized that thought causes all, you will know that there can never be limits on you that you yourself do not impose.

Nothing is impossible. All things are likely to happen. Whatever the mind can conceive, the mind can do. Whatever the mind conceives, the mind does.

THE MIGHTY TOOL

Form proceeds from mind, and mind controls all. This knowledge properly applied can change your life. You no longer need to batter circumstance and things; you no longer need to rail at the dealings of fate or frustrate your life against unwanted circumstance.

Everything proceeds from mind, everything proceeds from thought; and miracles are wrought in the quiet hours, and still rooms, when awakened souls harken their Divinity (Godlike character).

These thoughts of yours are far and away the most important thing you do. They are in fact the only thing you do. These thoughts of yours are the essence that makes form and brings circumstance. They are your sole tool with which to expand your consciousness.

There is nothing more important for you to do than carefully select those thoughts that you will think, those beliefs you will adopt, those attitudes you will take for your own, for by them you will be what you will be. Because of them you have arrived at exactly where you are today.

If you mean for your life to be progressive and full of achievement, health, love, and abundance, you will abandon each negative thought the moment it is presented to you.

You will refuse to accept any conception other than those that are in tune with good. If you think only positively than the universe will shower you with more good than you've ever dreamed. Therefore select your thoughts with care.

THE INFALLIBLE LAW

The law this book teaches works all of the time and nothing or nobody on the face of this earth can stop it from working. We didn't make this law. We neither start nor stop it.

Our only purpose here is to impart to you a knowledge of its existence and methods of using it. The law works 100% of the time. It never fails. If you apply it to achieve success and you meet with failure, it isn't the law that has failed-it is you.

You simply have failed to do the one thing that is necessary for you to obtain the slightest good and that is to think only positively of that good. If an opposite develops, it has developed because you have been more convinced of it then you have of the good you want. The law has still worked as it always must.

Thoughts are things. Awaken to your power over all. Cast aside your enemies: doubt, fear, and guilt. Ask and it shall be given; seek and ye shall find; knock and it shall be opened to you. You cannot dream a dream too big, nor aspire to high. Nothing is impossible. Everything which you can conceive and except is yours. Entertain no doubt. Refuse to accept worry or hurry or fear. That which knows and does everything is inside you and harkens to the slightest whisper.

Powerful Auto Suggestions:

- Right now the universe seeks to answer my every need.

- As I believe in my heart, so shall it be done unto me; this is the law of life and living.

- The God who made all creatures made no poor creature.

- Ask Yourself :
  "How is it that money comes so easily to me?"

- I need to only open my mind and my heart, keep my thoughts in the path of truth, and I am filled with the overflowing power, abundance, and love of the universe.

CHAPTER 5: INTUITION

In chapter five Andersen unveils the truth about our hearts. We have all heard the saying "Follow your heart" but most people do not take the time to understand the depth of that statement. We live in a world where our hearts rule and never the head. When we do follow our hearts, as a result success will come, health, love, peace, and a grander purpose will show up. Some of our opinions about life and ourselves have caused more pain than good. The only way to drown out this pain is to shine the light of truth.

"Everything we hear is opinion, not a fact. Everything we see is prospective, not the truth."

– Marcus Aurelius

INTUITION DEFINED

We are using the word intuition to cover a good deal more than the occurrence of "hunches." Under intuition we are classifying all the mysteries and apparently unexplainable phenomena which pass largely unnoticed in our world: clairvoyance, thought transference, contact with the spirit world, in addition to an instinctive grasp on the laws of construction (such as in mathematics and music).

Intuition describes our recognition and use of the great truth that mind is greater than matter and that the Universal Subconscious Mind contains the knowledge of all things and all times. It is the substance from which everything is made and is responsive to thought and desire.

A skeptical world cannot look away any longer. If records were kept of all phenomena, they would overflow the nation's libraries. The mechanistic and material age is passing.

Man is evolving into the age of the mind, wherein our dominion over the universe will shortly be achieved. Mind over matter; mind over time; as a result there will come a future of many dimensioned proportions with man at the center and yet encompassing all.

GENIUS

Thought transference, clairvoyance, the affecting of matter and circumstance through mind power, contact with the spirit world, are all results of the duality of the mind of man and the fact that the Universal Subconscious Mind responds to suggestion.

All the powers which might fall under the heading of intuition are possessed by the subconscious mind alone, but they are available only when controlled by the conscious mind.

The subconscious mind may see without eyes, hear without ears, leave the body to draw information and return again. It may see into the future, see into the past, form circumstance and matter. Its existence is independent of the body, for it lives in all things and it encompasses infinity. It is the soul of each person and the soul of the universe.

PERCEPTION OF UNIVERSAL LAW

Laws of construction, or rhythm, or movement are inherent in each of us. They are part and parcel of the Universal Subconscious Mind. Time moves in accordance with these laws.

Who has not been able to wake themselves from the sound sleep at an appointed hour simply because they consciously desired to before they went to sleep? Some never sleeping presence within us keeps an eye on the clock or simply on the movement of the universe, and if we desire to be awake by six, so we are.

Nature has fashioned us with the most reliable alarm clock of all, but our dependence upon mechanical devices dulls this faculty as it has dulled so many others. Did not Columbus himself sail toward the edge of the world which everyone said was flat? What else sustained him but his intuitive perception that the world was a sphere?

The universe moves and combines and builds according to certain fixed laws. These laws are part of the subconscious mind and are available to our perception if we will but clear away our doubts that is forever cluttering up our conscious minds.

"There is nothing more dreadful than the habit of doubt. It is a thorn that irritates and hurts; it is a sword that kills."

– Buddha

The bud of perfection in the seed of genius dwells within each of us. It comes to everyone in some quiet hour and whispers of the truth. Who has not felt the excited certainty of an impending event, a new idea, a useful business, a new invention, a theme for a novel, a sunset that demanded to be photographed, the foreknowledge of a friend's devotion, a loved one's high regard?

Who in their quiet hours, has not looked at the stars and felt peace, as deep within their soul the magnificent order of the universe's laws was for a while apparent?

THE INDWELLING BUD OF PERFECTION

Can we then, be the geniuses, even as those the world has known? The answer is that we not only can, but we are! Great genius lies dormant in each of us, waiting to be awakened.

We have to only take down the bars, unlock the door and invite our silent drawing forth. It is ourselves who have locked the genius within their prison, and the genius aspires to be set free. We build this cage and lock each time we say, "I'm not good enough," "I don't know how," "It's too hard for me," "I'm poor," "I'm tired," or "I'm nobody."

We make of this mighty mind a wimp, cowering in their cell, forced to act and create all of our negative fears and doubts into actuality and as a result to reduce the temple of the universe to a sorry, fumbling, fear-ridden speck upon the earth.

Geniuses we all shall be when we know and recognize and practice the truth. Not geniuses begotten by a whim of fate, but geniuses because we have controlled our destinies, geniuses because we moved in accord with the invincible power of an expanding universe.

FOLLOW THE HEART

This is a world in which the heart rules and never the head. The conscious mind of man has concerned itself with the frivolous ends of existence and has created a great lock against the powers of the subconscious mind.

The heart knows the truth of all things. It is the heart that is the seat of all intuition, our hope to arrive back home in the midst of and encompassing all the magnificent truth of our unlimited power.

Listen to the voice of your heart. Close your ears against the promptings of the conscious mind. The heart knows the way. In the inner most depths of your being it whispers the truth every minute of every day. Intuitively it proceeds. Intuitively it communicates. Leave to your conscious mind the doing of your daily tasks; leave to your heart the doing of that which is God's.

As you proceed you will find yourself being led more and more by your heart. When you feel the truth of a feeling that rises within you it will ask for no argument or examination. It will come to you as a whole thing, and you will ask no one whether it be fact or fiction, truth or fantasy, a good idea or poor. It will be a guiding light, and you will follow it, for it will have penetrated to your soul.

"The human heart feels things the eyes cannot see, and knows what the mind cannot understand."

–Robert Valett

"The heart has reasons that reasons cannot know."

– Blaise Pascal

It will be a great deal more than that which you may have termed a "hunch." It will be a great deal more than what you might have thought to be a "lucky guess." It will take deep root within your being and become one with you.

You will live life with unshakable strength and faith to see that it becomes the success, health, love, peace, or grander purpose that you desire in the world about you.

OUR GOALS

It is our intuitive perception of the laws of the universe that reveals to us God as he is. We need to only put all wishful thinking aside and save the desire to know the truth. Expectation and desire will light the way.

In the quietness of meditations the inner eye will see and the inner ear will hear, and the truth shall be revealed to us, and the truth shall make us free.

We will know that the way we lived yesterday has determined our today. We will know that the way we live today will determine our tomorrow. True intuition will be ours.

You are one with the intelligence of God. You need only to rub the dust from your eyes, clear your ear ways, and there becomes apparent a universe which has cradled you in everlasting arms, a universe that responds to your every mood, need, and desire.

Every soul that falls behind, another steps ahead. He who seeks will find; he who abandons the search as hopeless will find at once a hopeless life. It is a question of courage and effort, a question of desire.

We either work in accord with the power within us or by opposing it, destroy ourselves. It is for each person to decide. We are embarking on man's greatest age. An age in which the first movements are apparent to banish disease and suffering and poverty from the face of the earth - an age where brotherhood of man finally will arrive in peace and harmony.

Listen to the voice of the universe as it speaks within you. It is the voice of truth and it will guide you unerringly along the paths of your life. Deep within you there stands an immobile universe where all things and all law are revealed. Reach within this place of peace and quietness.

Listen to the voice of your heart. Close your eyes and sense a living, breathing universe dwelling within you. You are one with all people, all life, and all things. All of the limitless power of creation is yours to draw upon.

Know that the things of your life are the children of your thoughts, and your thoughts of today are now bearing the children of tomorrow. Allow all that is good. Refuse to accept all that is evil.

All that is and will ever be is available to all men and women. You need to only ask, allow, and it shall be given.

CHAPTER 6: FAITH

This chapter on Faith explains exactly why we are at the stages of life we now face. We have faith in a lot of things and unfortunately some are not benefiting our lives in the slightest. Faith in failure, faith in loss, faith in low self-esteem. Andersen shows the ways of achieving a Faith that will turn our lives into a glorious adventure, and how to allow all love, all kindness, joy, abundance, all health and all strength. In order for us to become Masters of our destiny we must harness this knowledge and use its power, for Faith gives power to a belief which as a result must manifest in the physical world.

"You cannot expect victory and plan for defeat. It's our Faith that activates the power of God."

– Joel Osteen

FAITH-THE MIGHTY TOOL

All things are rooted in faith. Even those of us who have the most difficulty applying this law to our daily lives will find innumerable instances in which we use it with perfect confidence.

We have faith in the air we breath, that the sun will rise, that the earth will revolve uniformly, that the stars will maintain their places in the heavens. We have faith in our own existence yet we admit we know the cause of none of these.

Our faith is blind! How strange it is that we so often scoff at faith in the less tangible fields of human existence. Faith led Columbus to the West Indies, Galileo to the stars, Democritus to the atom, Magellan around the world. These men departed from the beaten paths and followed their visions, and all the world has benefited from their faith. Faith is the single most important tool of our existence.

RETURNING TO THE SUBCONSCIOUS

What ever the conclusions the Conscious Mind forwards to the Subconscious Mind, the latter immediately returns in physical reality, for the law of its own nature is to become what ever it knows.

As a result our thoughts become things and we can neither start or stop the process; we can only control our thinking. We are now able to see why it is that faith is such an important tool in the molding and determining of our lives.

Faith is simply that factor which gives the power of conviction to a thought and as a result impresses the thought upon the Subconscious Mind as a conclusion which must be manifested in the physical world. Anything you are convinced of must become real in your life, for thought plus faith creates.

FAITH IS AFFIRMATION

If the Subconscious Mind receives your conviction that you have money, you will have money. If it receives your conviction that you have health, you will have health. If the Subconscious Mind receives your conviction that you have love, you will have love. If it receives your conviction that you are successful, you will be successful. If it receives your conviction that you are wise, you will have wisdom.

What ever the premise, the Subconscious Mind will create it into physical reality. See how simple such a premise may be: "I have money," only that, and money is manifested.

Why is it that we have such difficulty in doing this simple thing? It is because we lack faith. It is because the thing we want is expressed as hope, and in a million different ways throughout the day we affirm our faith in the very opposite direction.

ALL DECISION IS ACCEPTANCE

You've got to think success to be successful. No one was ever successful by thinking failure. NO one was ever a failure by thinking success. It IS that simple. And the tool which we must use to prevent negative circumstances from entering our lives is that of faith.

You must reaffirm to yourself the fact that you are to be a successful person and know that a power greater than you is directing you in the correct path. You must understand that it is not up to you to determine the ways and means and exact sequence of events by which you are to attain your end.

You must understand that the great Subconscious Mind, or God, will affect its own ways and means and time in which to accomplish it.

"Faith is to believe what you do not see; the reward of this faith is to see what you believe."

– Saint Augustine

ISOLATION BRINGS FEAR

We human beings are creatures of little faith. We isolate ourselves from God, from the roots of our being. The reins of destiny are in our own hands.

All things, good and evil, have their beginnings in faith, and as you believe, so shall it be done unto you. We shall have our beliefs anyway; why not make them good, in the fine ends of man, in abundance, in health, in strength, in integrity? Let us use the word Faith to mean the overcoming of negative thought.

Let us use the word delusion to mean belief in negative circumstance and negative thinking. Let us refuse to accept delusion. Let us take up Faith like a sword, and by using it, overcome all things. The Subconscious Mind, then, turns physical reality into each of our beliefs.

We isolates ourselves from God, from our sense of unity with the infinite intelligence; then, feeling like a small and lonely animal in a vast universe, we supposes that the responsibility for all things in our own life depends upon our own physical action.

POWER THROUGH UNION

No one can consistently exercise faith in all aspects of their life without the secure knowledge that God is with them every minute of every day.

Unless you are willing to give up your problems and turn them over to God, you will find that you are making very poor solutions of them indeed.

You will feel your own inadequacy at every turn in the road and will shortly be projecting more failure than success into the Subconscious Mind. Make up your mind right now that there isn't the slightest use trying to do anything by yourself.

"The drop of water becomes of supreme usefulness by losing itself in the ocean."

–James Allen

The millions of facts and circumstances beyond your understanding make of you a microbe on the face of the earth the moment you isolate yourself from the Subconscious Mind and say, "I can do this all by myself."

Join forces with the Subconscious Mind and the entire universe speeds to answer your every need. For this wise and omnipotent father knows of your every need before you voice it, and may affect instantaneous manifestation in your life of whatever it is you are convinced of.

The Subconscious Mind contains the knowledge of all ways and means and times, and you may rest your problem there with the surety that it will be answered with perfection.

Do not keep examining the pot to see if the water is boiling. You don't have to double-check God. Don't make up your mind that your path should lead in a certain direction and then be disturbed because you find it is leading elsewhere. Know that your every step is unerringly guided on a perfect route to your destination.

THE PERFECT PARTNER

When you take up the full knowledge of your partnership with God, you will find splendor in everything you touch. You will see an ordered universe rushing to do your bidding. You will see the design of all things fitted to your every need.

You will know that the senior partner is the one who carries out every decision, an infallible executive who never makes a mistake. You will begin to see yourself as a beloved son or daughter who needs only to ask and it shall be given.

You will make each of your decisions clear and without contradiction, and you will hold them with complete confidence until they have arrived in your world to answer your call.

You will have the courage and faith of your convictions and will reject all else until your desires become manifest in your life. In this sense of oneness with God you will never be alone, and all the power of the universe will dwell within you. You will no longer have to fight for faith; faith will be as natural as breathing. Act as if it were impossible to fail.

CIRCUMSTANCE VERSES FAITH

Because our conscious minds keep insisting that the physical world around us is final reality, we must use faith to regain our spiritual values. You must use faith to rise above negative circumstance, and you must never fall victim to that which goes on around you.

Refuse to be trapped into believing that the cause of anything exists on the physical plane. Have complete confidence in the fact that first cause is mental and first cause once set in motion must inevitably manifest itself in the physical world.

Do not deny any negative circumstance. Simply have faith in what you believe and refuse to accept negative circumstance as final. This is the proper use of faith. For faith will overcome the deluded convictions of the conscious mind, build habits of positive thinking, which is the first step on the road to power.

POSITIVE THINKING

Faith is nothing other than sustained effort to impart to the Universal Subconscious Mind that thought which you wish to be manifested in your experience. Faith means thinking the one thing and not thinking of its opposite.

Faith means refusing to accept any negative circumstance or to entertain any negative thought. Faith means complete reliance and trust in the power and goodness of God, and absolute trust that whatever you conceive with conviction will be returned to you in this world!

There is no end to the power of positive thinking. As long you are banishing negative thoughts from your mind you will be caught up in the entire expanding power of the universe.

You may have in your mind all of the knowledge that exists in our libraries, but unless you become a positive thinker you will meet with nothing but failure in your life. No matter how you choose to think, you are calling into existence those very things you believe in.

The choice is then simple: good or evil. No sane person understanding this will dally with their choice.

BREAKING THE BAD HABIT

Breaking negative thinking requires measures as sure as a surgeon's knife. It is a procedure, confined entirely to the mind and spirit, which we will ask you to adopt for the next 30 days.

You are not to accept a single negative thought nor dwell on a single negative premise. This does not mean that such thoughts or ideas will not occur to you. They most certainly will occur. You simply will have to refuse to accept any of them, discarding them immediately as they occur, as fictional ideas.

By deliberately planting only positive seeds in the garden of the Subconscious Mind, you will not only set about in eventual harvesting of the greatest crop of good ever to enter your life, but more important, you will be building up a habit of positive thinking that will become easier and easier, day by day.

Eventually, you will no longer have to struggle with positive and negative, truth and illusion. You will ally yourself with the forces for good in the universe and achieve an attunement and an effortlessness in life that once seemed impossible of imagining.

THE MENTAL DIET

This is going to be no easy time, discarding every negative thought for a period of 30 days, but it is something you absolutely must do. Until you become master of your thinking, you will never become master of your fate.

If you fall from the path of your resolve and entertain negative thoughts, become depressed, there is nothing to do but start over. It is exceptionally important that you do this thing. Let nothing stand in your way.

You will be training your mind to obey rather than you obey it. You will be developing the habit of concentration as well as the habit of positive thinking.

WE CHOOSE THOUGHTS

Like the writer who authors a story, each of us authors our own life by our choice of what thoughts we will accept and which we will reject.

Each of our lives is a story, unfolded by the silent contemplative author who dwells within us who does nothing more than accept and reject, who is involved only in making choices. And each of these choices is manifested in the physical world.

We are today living testimonies to the choices we have made from the thoughts that have streamed through our minds. We are literally products of the thoughts we have chosen to accept. We are what we believe we are, that only, nothing more nothing less.

"Every thought we think is creating our future."

–Louise Hay

"Whether you think you can, or think you can't. You're right." –Henry Ford

We have assured the indwelling self that it can be anything it accepts and has faith in. We are deliberately compelling ourselves to accept all love, all kindness, all joy, all abundance, all health, and all strength.

We are teaching ourselves to accept only good. We are saying nothing is true but the great and the good and the beautiful. Only these we will add unto ourselves.

WHO IS "I"

Ask yourself who this observer is that you refer to as "I." It is not thought. It is not body. It simply observes. It is neither past or present or future, but simply exists. Here is your true being. Here is your real self.

In your daily practice of thought control, when you have slowed down the thought stream after relaxation and breath control, turn always to the Self that dwells deep within you.

Find the point of consciousness from where all things are but observations. The arrival at this point of consciousness is the attainment of "the peace that passeth all understanding" and is the position from which all things are possible, without effort, without exercising of will, but simply through contemplation and choice.

"People often say motivation doesn't last – Well neither does bathing–that's why we recommended daily."

–Zig Ziglar

Things to remember to do during our 30 day mental diet: We will first reject all negative thoughts and refuse to add them to ourselves. We will entertain only positive thoughts of abundance, joy, love, kindness, and success.

We will daily engage in a period of thought control which we will achieve with the aid of breathing exercises, always aiming at arriving at that point of consciousness where all things and thoughts are a matter of observation.

This will prove to be one of the most rewarding times of your life. Not only because of the manifestations you meet within the physical world, but also because of the towering sense of peace and strength that will come to you as soon as you get to know the magnificence that is yours.

You will sense all of the unity of all things, come to understand that nothing is done by man alone but all things are done by the Universal Subconscious Mind, or the mind of God.

You will understand that you have nothing to do but decide each of the issues of your life and put your faith and trust in the wisdom and omnipotence of this all-knowing mind.

"Your imagination is your preview of life's coming attractions."   – Albert Einstein

LEAVE IT TO GOD

Perhaps the most difficult thing each of us has to learn is to "Let go and let God." As long as we keep our problems with us, dwelling on each aspect of them, we are defeating our own ends.

The mighty power of the Universal Subconscious Mind, recognizing our command that we are determined to do things by ourselves, filters into our lives in a tiny trickle over the dam we have built against it.

But once you turn your problem over to the Universal Mind with the request, "Here you handle it," the dam is removed and the stream flows and miracles appear before our very eyes. Such miracles that we can only wonder with awe at how lucky we are or how beneficent are the circumstances that surround us.

DO NOT DWELL ON YOUR PROBLEMS

Never keep any problem in your mind for more than a few minutes a time. Consider the issues and possible paths or courses of action you might take.

If you cannot decide what to do, turn the problem over to the Subconscious with the sure knowledge that the correct answer will be returned to you. Forget about your problem altogether, secure in the knowledge that its execution rests in the most capable hands in the universe.

The answers to your problems will burst upon you like a light. It's very likely you will chastise yourself for not having been aware of the answers before. It will suddenly seem so simple.

FAITH IS TRUST

Where ever we go, what ever we do, we must always know that the Subconscious Mind is our mighty and invisible partner. The Subconscious is our executive vice president, our crew and staff, advisor and confessor.

He requires complete trust and confidence, and once he sets about a task we have given him we must leave everything up to him. Interference at any point He interprets as meaning a new goal, and He immediately sets about achieving this new one instead.

We will find that His nature is to wind things up jig time and in the most marvelous manner. Once we have completely given over to Him anyone of our problems, and have been witness to the manner in which He solves it, we will never again doubt or disbelieve.

Our job is not to figure out the "how." The "how" will show up out of the commitment and belief in the "what."

–Jack Canfield

"You cannot have a positive life and a negative mind. Put your expectations on God, not on people."

–Joyce Meyer

FAITH VERSES HOPE

One of the traps we so often fall into is the confusion of hope with faith. Hope has scarcely any relation to faith at all, and nevertheless is a frail instrument needed for moving the Subconscious Mind.

Hope is a pessimist looking at things optimistically. Hope is a whiny wish for something better. It is no wonder that those who seek to better their lives through hope are very seldom witness to improvements.

Most of us set about the projects of our lives with hope instead of faith. Hope is a dimly perceived light, now flickering faintly in the darkness, now obscured by the gloom. Hope is wishing. Faith on the other hand is a radiance that bathes all things in illumination. Faith is knowing.

What ever we know to be fact we have complete faith in. You know the lights will go on when you throw the switch because you have tried it before and it works. As a result you have complete faith.

Yet the methods by which electricity is picked up in generators, transmitted over lines, distributed to your homes and finally achieves the miracle of light by heating a tiny filament in a vacuum sealed transparent glass globe are most probably little-known to you.

Similarly, on the intangible plains of human existence we need not achieve full knowledge of why and how everything works and is constructed. We need only to try working with spiritual law, discover that it works, and come into complete faith through knowing.

"Just trust that everything is unfolding the way it is supposed to. Don't resist. Surrender to what is, let go of what was, and have faith in what will be. Great things are waiting for you around the corner."

– Sonia Ricotti

"If you change the way you look at things, the things you look at change."
–Dr. Wayne Dyer

FAITH IS MENTAL LAW

It sometimes sounds extremely childish to say to a person who is distraught with problems and grief that they may overcome them by simply having faith. Faith is knowing, and at that moment they cannot know.

Only by communion with the indwelling self, the quiet assured place in the recesses of their being will they come into the possession of true knowledge and this will allow them to have faith.

One person can never insist with success that another person have faith. Nor can any person insists that they themselves have faith when they are troubled by doubt and fear.

Faith only comes through knowledge in the general rules that are contained in the pages of this book. Your daily meditations with the indwelling "I" will bring this knowledge home with full force and achieve for you a faith that will turn life into a glorious adventure.

Knowledge without faith is like a ship without a sea. It may be beautiful to behold, but it does very little good. Do the work. Keep the faith!

What ever you choose is yours. What ever you reject shall never touch you. You need to only accept and allow. All things will be added unto you by a power which leaps to acknowledge your faith and your decisions.

CHAPTER 7: ATTRACTION

Chapter seven is a very powerful chapter for all of us to study and understand. Andersen describes in detail the power that each and every one of us has within and how to obtain it. He also teaches us how we can use this power to modify and change our very circumstances. We will learn as we hold on to the thoughts of what we want, we start calling on one of the greatest laws of the universe, and as we do this our dreams and desires become our reality. Not only will, but there is no way they cannot.

"Your present circumstances don't determine where you can go; they merely determine where you start."

–Nido Qubein

THE ENDLESS PRAYER

The human being is a center of life force, attracting some things, repelling others, according to their beliefs. It is the nature of any unit built from Universal Subconscious Mind to attract unto itself those thought-things that answer the mental vibrations it exudes.

Intelligence responds to intelligence, and thought creates vibrations which inevitably attract the thing in the image. What you pay attention to grows. This powerful knowledge can be used to direct your thoughts to create your life's desires. We have the ability to create consistent positive thoughts whenever we choose.

The one mind in which we all live contains an infinite number of possibilities, all of which are capable of becoming manifest in space and time when the conception has been planted in the Universal Subconscious Mind.

What ever you choose and accept must develop in your experience because it is attracted to you by an irresistible and immutable law. A law which isn't working some of the time, or occasionally, but every second of the day.

Whether we like analogy or not, we are literally praying every minute of our lives, and every single one of our prayers are answered. There is no escaping this wheel of answered thought and belief. It is the law of life.

What ever has developed in our experience has not been brought to us by luck or coincidence, but simply a physical manifestation of our thought and belief. Whether it has brought us good or evil, it is in effect an answered prayer.

You are what you think; you can attract what you think. Your life is a product of your thought and belief. Nothing in the world can change this fact. To alter your life the only single course open is to alter your thinking.

THE PRIMAL FORCE

Attraction manifests a high order of design and intelligence. Science has chosen to call it the Laws of Nature while religion has chosen to call it God. We for the purposes of new definition, call it the Universal Subconscious Mind.

Studying the lines of force of a magnet, science has discovered that these lines never cross. They either repel or attract one or the other. No matter how far a magnet is displaced from the lines of force in a free field, it will always return to its point of balance.

It is the same with the mind that sets up certain patterns of thought. Everything contrary to this thought is automatically repelled. Everything relating to this thought is automatically attracted.

No matter how far such a mind is away from those things which it seeks, it will return to them as it must.

It is never material things that makes success; it is the thinking of man. A conditioned habit of prosperity thinking is usually ingrained on the mind of a person who is born into wealth. As a consequence, they seem to attract further wealth to themselves effortlessly.

Similarly those born into poverty must exercise the greatest perseverance before wealth smiles on them, for they must gradually condition their minds to think positively of money before money will be manifested. Each small success that comes their way contributes to building favorable thought patterns of confidence and faith.

The indisputable fact is this: those things that a conscious organism believes are always returned by the Universal Subconscious Mind.

ATTRACTION IS EVERYWHERE

The very earth itself exudes a magnetism that steadies the needle of the compass at sea and delicately counter balances the centrifugal force of the earth's path around the sun.

Dynamic attraction is everywhere present in the universe. Call it what you will-magnetism, polarity, electricity, thought power-it is everywhere attraction.

A magnet may attract iron and have no effect on aluminum. You yourself may attract loss and repel gain, but there ends the comparison between physical and mental law.

The magnet itself cannot change its properties of attraction, while you, by changing your thought and belief, can set up an entirely new field of magnetism, and attract those very things that you were repelling before.

STEPPING STONES TO THE STARS

It is sheer vanity expressing discontentment having been born into lack and limitation, while someone else has been born into abundance. When you have truly come to understand that there is only one mind that is in all things, you will know the difference between you and any other person is purely illusionary.

Your "I" may have known lack and limitation, but when you cast these negations out and take on the knowledge of abundance and health, your "I" has changed and you are no longer the same person.

True, you still occupy the same body, but even as your surroundings will swiftly change, so your body will become vigorous and unafraid, purposeful, animated by the greatest power in the universe.

You can be anything you want to be and do anything you want to do. Born high or born low makes not the slightest difference. We are all born equal for we are one. Those who dispute this point suffer from pride, and pride kills quicker than the highly poisonous plant of Socrates.

"We live in a world with all good things. So great is the abundance of spiritual, mental and material blessings that every man and woman on this globe could not only be provided with every necessary good, but could live in the midst of abounding plenty, and yet have so much to spare."

–James Allen

VANITY – THE KILLER

It is vanity, isolated ego, pride, which is our undoing. It's "I have to do this," "I have to do that," when the truth is that the "I" does nothing but choose and except and all things are done by the Universal Subconscious Mind.

When a person lets go of their vanity, sees their unity with all life and all things, rejects personal isolation, then they invite the great power into their life, and all things are arranged according to the good they desire.

The majority of us act as if the most important thing in all life is to get the best of our neighbors, better clothes, better cars, and better jobs. We frustrate ourselves with our isolated egos and spill out our energies on the relentless blade of competition.

We set out to deal with the world as if it were an enemy set out to hurt us, and the world turns out to be exactly what we conceive it to be, as it always must.

Man's gravest error was the decision to isolate ourselves from God, or the Universal Subconscious Mind, in which all things have their being and in which all power is contained.

ACKNOWLEDGING THE SENIOR PARTNER

The successful and vigorous person cannot be vain; if you become so you will be shortly reduced to failure. "I did it all by myself," and down you come again.

Humility regained and the Subconscious Mind again allowed to enter your life, you once more begin the climb through another set of "fortunate circumstances".

Some people have ridden this whirlgig 8 or 9 times and still are no wiser for it. This you can rest assured of: the really great and outstanding people of our world have a constant partner - God or the Subconscious Mind, which ever you will; and this partner is consulted on all matters and is acknowledged to be the doer of all their deeds. They attune themselves to all the power of creation when they acknowledge the God within.

LET GO AND LET GOD

Overcoming vanity and relaxing into mental attitudes of trust and confidence often have been expressed in the metaphysical saying, "Let go and let God." Yet it would seem from observation of many who quote this saying that they haven't absorbed it.

On the one hand, they say, "I trust in God," and on the other, they act as if God were quite untrustworthy. They set out for certain goals, and except the image. But the very first time they observed that the path they are following doesn't coincide with the route they believe they should take, they are convinced that God has made a mistake or hasn't heard them in the first place.

You can't predict the Subconscious Mind, and you can't outguess it. If you try, you defeat those very things you have set out to do.

The Subconscious Mind always works with perfect knowledge of all times and all places, all people and all things. Only God knows the way a thing may be done; and man never will.

Whatever you conceive and except with faith will be yours regardless of the apparently longer paths and roads you must follow to its attainment.

The road you are guided to take is the only way, there is no other, and as long as you work with the Subconscious Mind your steps and routes are perfect.

THE INVINCIBLE GUIDE

"Let go and let God" means to trust God, to trust in the perfect knowledge of the Subconscious Mind, to know what ever paths you travel toward your goals are the right ones, the only ones, the perfect ones, for you have been set upon them by the Omni potent mind of God which makes no mistakes and will deliver you safely and prepared at your destination.

This means to do nothing but observe and accept, and what ever you accept is delivered to you by the Subconscious Mind. There is no personal responsibility for anything but thought, for accepted thoughts become manifest in the physical world.

"Our job is to hold on to the thoughts of what we want, make it absolutely clear in our minds what we want, and from that we start to invoke one of the greatest laws in the universe, and that's the law of attraction. You become what you think about most, but you also attract what you think about most. Keep those thoughts positive!"

–John Assaraf

AWAY WITH VANITY AND GUILT

Cast aside your vanity (pride). You do nothing by yourself, and you are never alone. All things are done by the Universal Subconscious Mind, which is always right where you are.

You are not isolated from the world; you are a part of it and at the same time the whole of it. The world is your friend if you are friendly with yourself.

Cast aside your guilt. Who does not make mistakes? Do not feel guilty for mistakes, for it is this path we must travel to become one with God.

Guilt has no place in life. Mistakes are for learning. Guilt holds onto mistakes and make them happen again. Guilt isolates you from the Subconscious Mind. Guilt brings about vanity, the vanity of being alone, without God.

Feel your unity with all things and you will see vanity slip away. There is no past, no future, only a present that is always existing, and you will feel guilt dissolve. God is in you, has done what you have done, and God does not chastise himself, nor destroy himself. Shame and remorse are poisonous to the subconscious. Allow them to enter your life no more.

"Without pain, there would be no suffering, without suffering we would never learn from our mistakes. To make it right, pain and suffering is the key to all windows, without it, there is no way of life."

–Angelina Jolie

"The more grateful we fix our minds on the supreme when good things come to us, the more good things we receive, and the more rapidly they will come; and the reason simply is that the mental attitude of gratitude draws the mind into closer touch with the source from which the blessings come."

–Wallace D. Wattles

There is absolutely only one way to make the law work in your favor, and that is to trust it completely and not predict it.

"You say to God, "I have never seen you provide for me."

God says to you, "You have never trusted me."

–Corallie Buchanan

IN EVERY OBSTACLE – OPPORTUNITY

When you have learned to trust the law completely, you will begin to see every delay and every obstacle as opportunities. You will become fit and ready for what awaits you when you arrive at your destination.

There is no such thing as failure unless it is accepted. There is no such thing as defeat unless it is accepted. There is no such thing as evil unless it is accepted.

Except you're appointed tasks and circumstances with complete faith that they will provide the perfect path to the attainment of your desires. Failure, defeat, evil and disease can not touch you if you will refuse to accept them. Only what you accept comes to you.

All else is but temporary and merely a step to your goal. Do not keep examining your goal to see if you have attained it. "A watched pot never boils" for the simple reason that you are watching it when it isn't boiling, and this is the thought you project into the Subconscious Mind.

Rest assured of the eventual accomplishment of your goal and take pleasure and wisdom from each experience along the way. If life were only moments of victory, it would be very short indeed. Learn to enjoy the journey.

THOUGHT ATMOSPHERE

The Universal Subconscious Mind denies us nothing. Nature denies us nothing. We always get exactly what we ask for. There is no lack, failure, or despair which we do not create for ourselves in our own minds.

It is just as simple, in fact downright simpler, to create abundance and success and health in our minds and therefore experience them in the physical world.

NO LIMITATION

There are no limitations for God. There is no lack in the Universal Subconscious Mind. Whatever you dare ask for will be given; and you will need only ask and have faith.

Become infused with the Observer, the great contemplator, the immortal "I." Each of us has no responsibility other than our thoughts and our beliefs.

FIRST CAUSE

Nobody achieves anything by "going out and getting it." The very premise insinuates at the outset that you believe whatever you are after belongs to somebody else and you have to "take it away."

When you have created on the plane of mind the conviction that whatever you are after is already yours, you will be guided to the proper paths and the proper action that will achieve this goal.

Action of itself alone produces nothing. True action will dissolve a mountain. True action is neither more or less than true thought, for action follows thought. If your thought is true, your action will be impeccably guided by the Subconscious Mind.

HOW TO USE YOUR WILL

All effort should be aimed at attunement with Universal Mind, at arriving at a point of consciousness where you have complete faith and trust in the infinite power.

Do not direct your will toward the physical world. It avails you nothing, and in the end defeats you. However, there is one very important place for you to exercise your will, and that is in your choice of thoughts.

Will to think right only and not to change objects and circumstances of your physical world through thought power or physical action.

Deliberately choose to think only those thoughts which are in the image of your true desire. Refuse to accept any others. By this correct application of the will on the mental plane, the outside world grows into the image of your desire.

"Every thought we think is creating our future."

–Louise Hay

"Create the highest, grandest vision for your life, because you become what you believe."

–Oprah Winfrey

ATTRACTION IS MENTAL CHOICE

What ever you choose to think is sent to you from the Universal Intelligence. These thoughts, once accepted by you, will manifest in the physical world.

What will you think? The choice is yours and yours alone. It's the only true choice you will ever have in life. Hell or heaven are your choices you make for yourself. The greatest adventure in life is to come to know the Universal Mind for its infinite power, and to learn how to use this power to fill our lives with good and abundance.

At the end of such a path lies a magnificent spiritual awakening, a transfiguration and the key to life's mysteries.

THE REAL YOU

Don't confuse what you seem to be with what you really are. To the real you, the indwelling self, the observer in the depths of your soul, nothing is impossible.

What you seem to be is merely a fraction of what you really are. Refuse to think of yourself as a name, as a holder of a certain job, as a person who resides in a certain town, in a certain country, as a person with a certain history. That is what you seem to be.

In the solitude of a quiet room, next to a river, overlooking the ocean, turn your thoughts within to the real you. Slow down your breathing until you feel complete peace and relaxation. Retreat into the depths of your being until your very thoughts are things observed.

Ask yourself, "Who is this that observes?" The real you is a mighty truth, a loud and clear call in the greatest age of man.

Let the spiritual element rule your life. Give each of your problems to the Universal Sub conscious Mind and listen for the answer. When the answer comes, accept it with complete faith and confidence.

Close your mind to all lack and limitation. Into your consciousness come the most important of all things – your thoughts. They come not to visit you but to take root and make themselves known as the physical things of your life.

"All you have to do is plant the seed in your mind, care for it, work steadily toward your goal, and it will become a reality. Not only will but there is no way it cannot. You see, that's a law."

–Earl Nightingale

Affirmations:

- I am now allowing my desires to come into fruition.

- There is no limit to abundance, and the universe provides me with all I need.

- I know the real truth and the real power is within me.

- What I accept God creates.

"A man by himself is a microbe. A man attuned to his inner self is a universe."

–U.S. Andersen

Strength, health and abundance are yours. The universe has an infinite supply. Your every decision is answered from a perfect and inexhaustible source of power.

CHAPTER 8: LOVE

Chapter eight will reopen your heart to Love. Andersen describes the pureness of Love and how important a part it plays in our everyday lives. Seeing everything with the eyes of Love will open new doors and banish the feelings of fear and discontentment. Love is in each of us and in this chapter you will learn that you need not drive for Love because Love is what you already are.

"The essence of creativeness is Love of life, for such Love guides a man to do something better or bigger or more enlightening than he has ever done before. Seek Love above all things, for we have known absolute Love and are lost without it."

–U.S. Andersen

LOVE GOVERNS ALL

Much has been written and said for love. Poets have praised it; musicians have sung about it; plays and stories are ever unfolding its many-sided drama.

"Here is the truth about love" they say, and present a romantic love, but a half-truth only and nearly all the world is deluded. The surging, welling, emotional searching that throbs within each human heart can never be reduced only to a relationship between men and women.

The home and marriage provide release for our sex drive and the reproductive necessities of society, but neither of these very admirable institutions is in any way a school for love. For no one can love another unless they first love humanity.

Love is all. God is love. It is the nature of our basic unity, the underlying dim remembrance of complete spiritual oneness that keeps us forever seeking union with others.

From Universal Mind we have been differentiated into separateness, isolated within a fleshy prison, and throughout our incarnation in life we reach out to receive and to give and to come together – to return again to complete unity.

Beauty, courage, loyalty, perseverance, and creation are all born of love successfully given and received. Distortion, fear, unfair behavior, hate, resentment, violence, and failure are all born of love frustrated. And so it is that love governs all – the supreme law of life.

THE CONSTANT SEARCH

Love we seek above all things, for we have known absolute love and are lost without it. All of our hurts are received when we are reaching for love and we are rejected. As a result the prompters of the Subconscious Mind are then planted by the pain remembrances of our love rejections.

In our separateness, we long for our unity that rests at the most important part of our Subconscious, and this is our motivating force, love. According to how we are able to give and receive it, all things in life come to us.

SPIRITUAL UNITY

The denial of love is fear, and fear is the father to hate, and are the seeds from which all wrong doing grows. Is it any wonder, then, that love will overcome all, for with love there is no fear, and with love there is no wrong doing, with love there is no opposition.

True love then is simply recognition of the spiritual unity of all life. Once you have realized that you and your neighbor are one it is no longer possible for you to perform an inappropriate act against them because it would be as if you performed it against yourself.

Anyone who regards life as a battle, who seeks to beat others or destroy them, is doing neither more nor less than beating or destroying themselves. One! One! One! Sings the Universe.

"We are only as strong as we are united, as weak as we are divided."

–J.K. Rowling

We are all sprung from one intelligence. We all return to one intelligence. There is but one immortal underlying Self to all creation. Separated from it in our bodies, we desire to know this complete unity again, and it is to this emotional drive that we give the name love.

HATE AND LOVE

Few will dispute the power of love, but the vast majority of us have difficulty bringing it into all aspects of our lives.

Hundreds of buried pain remembrances, or prompters, have set up coping mechanisms within our Subconscious so that we automatically are directed to greet certain circumstances or things or people with aggression, cruelty, fear, timidity, or a thousand different other negations that backfire on us daily.

Yet all of these prompters can be dissolved by meditation at the center of consciousness, by finding the Kingdom of Heaven. At this magic center, where all things are known and understood, absolute love will banish fear and hate.

Prompters of the Subconscious must be dealt with at the roots of their beings. All negative thinking and fear and hate must be cast out of the mind by choice at the center of consciousness.

ABSOLUTE LOVE WITHIN

Love is the supreme law, for through it we throw off the bonds of separateness and see the great spiritual unity in which we have our being

You are never separate from your wife or husband, neighbor or friend. Through love we attain a unity with all. We do not have to drive for love. Love is in us, complete and absolute.

Love cries out for expression from the very depths of our being, but we lock it in. We consider it smart and adult to build a fence around love and submit to loneliness, pride and vanity. We hurt only ourselves.

Those who deprive themselves of the expression of love, deprive themselves of all things. Love moves through the universe, expressing itself through every flower, tree, cloud and raindrop and needs no one for its fulfillment. Love makes the world flourish. It will flourish your life too if you just let it!

"The one thing we can never get enough of is Love. And the one thing we never give enough of is Love."

–Henry Miller

CREATION SPRINGS FROM LOVE

Life is creation, and creation is a labor of love. Nothing springs from the vast creativeness of the Universal Subconscious Mind unless there is first a desire to contribute to the community.

The essence of creativeness is love of life, for such love guides a person to do something better or bigger or more enlightening than they have ever done before.

Such love catches a person in the great unity and the great purpose, and they instinctively perceive the direction in which life moves, becomes one with its efforts, contributes, and creates.

Life seeks for knowledge, and creation is a measure of what has been learned. Creation is the purpose of life, and creation springs from love. Each of us has talent, sometimes several, given especially to us, for through us God has become something unique in the universe.

Love develops our talents, sets us free to do the special work that we can do. No matter what else we do in life, we are never completely happy unless our talents are developed, unless our destinies are fulfilled, unless we enlarge the vision and knowledge of God which all humanity strives.

By allowing love to work in our lives as a power for good, we become free to develop our special gifts in accord with an expanding and seeking universe.

We become free to develop our talents, and we become free to contribute. This contribution, when it is individualized, advances all humanity along the road of knowledge and in turn moves in accord with the very nature of life itself.

"When I stand before God at the end of my life, I would hope that I would not have a single bit of talent left, and I could say, "I used everything you gave me."

–Erma Bombeck

The perfect seed of success and happiness lies within each of us, and there is a channel in each of us through which it may become perfectly expressed. This channel in every case is opened only by love, and nothing may close it but the lack of love.

LOVE OR DIE

Love is the motivating law of life. On all sides of us we see the unstoppable command of the universe; "Love or die." Through the love we serve, and by serving we multiply abundance and good, knowledge, beauty and comfort.

Through the lack of love we grow selfish and bitter and we sow the seeds of hate and destruction. By working with love we add all things unto ourselves and add all things unto humanity.

God is love. Therefore, the great teachings he is showing us is that all humanity dwells in love and love dwells in all humanity. All things good, great and small, are a labor of love. It does not do anyone any good to recognize the laws of "thoughts become things," if they do not have love.

Despite all their will to think positively and to except only good they will find their thinking warped into patterns of selfishness, bitterness and resentment every time they are faced with a crisis in life.

If love has not made itself fully known to a person, this person sees a hostile world about them and regards other people as hostile creatures bent on beating them or destroying them or taking from them.

As long as this type of belief lies at the decisive part of their subconscious, they are creating an environment exactly the opposite of that which they wish to have. Love never fails.

OPEN YOUR HEART

It seems so difficult for us to open our hearts to love. We are so mindful of our petty hurts and rejections. We are so pulled into our own little problems and victories and failures so in turn we isolate ourselves from the great unity.

Like hurt animals we lie in lonely retreat and lick our fancied wounds; and always rebuild our walls. Walls to protect us from further hurt. Far from protecting us, our walls visit upon us the greatest hurt of all, for by them we slowly kill ourselves, not only physically, but mentally and spiritually as well.

Open your heart. Allow love to enter. What matters a hurt when it is but a step toward fulfillment? Life is for the living and some experience of pain and sorrow is essential to distinguish between pleasure and joy.

"Love heals the body, comforts the lonely hour, illumines the darkest path, redeems from sin and evil, brings prosperity, overcomes fear, builds character and reveals the meaning of life."

–Walter Chalmers

LOVE OR SUFFER

As individuals in this great God seeking drama we know as life, we have but two main choices: Love or suffer! Love fuses all beings and all life into a great common purpose: to share and contribute and advance along the common path toward God.

All of the evil prompters of the subconscious mind are buried memories of love rejections and love frustrations. They form dams that prohibit the free flow of love through our consciousness. They cause bitterness, fear and hate and they bring evil into our world in opposition to that which we consciously desire.

THE FRUSTRATIONS OF LOVE

The perfect seed of love is within. Perfect love is in each of us constantly seeking outlet. All we have to do is let it. We all depend on each other for our very existence. People have not advanced by fighting, hating and competition, but by being one at labor toward a common goal.

Love is always trying to express infinite good through you. Look with the eyes of love, listen with the ears of love, speak with the tongue of love, think with the mind of love, and feel with the heart of love.

LOVE AND SEXUALITY

The most important love expression of mankind is sexuality. In this relation between men and women, in the sexual act, is expressed the complete physical and spiritual hunger of one being for another.

No other activity or expression of mankind provides such a tool outlet for love as sex. Yet how little it is understood, and how abused! The end and aim of the sex act is not only for procreation – it is the expression of love.

The emotional search of each man and woman, to give and receive, to possess and be possessed, is fully realized in the sex act when there is a free flow of unselfish love between the partners.

It is sexuality that provides us with a human outlet and a human expression of divine love. A persons sex life will be an expression of love or it won't be, and if not they are out of tune with life, and their dissatisfaction is but a symptom.

THE DESIRE FOR FUSION

Love is the recognition of our true being and the dim remembrance of the complete unity from which we have sprung. Love is the great motivation to re-experience this unity. Love is the desire of fusion.

There is no such thing as being promiscuous when love is present. Promiscuous sexual contacts are always the symptom of a person who's lost from love and is endlessly seeking fulfillment through varied sexual experiences.

People who choose this type of lifestyle are doomed to external disappointment until they discover that satisfactory experience is the result of love and never the cause.

THE GREAT FULFILLMENT

We are monogamous creatures because we need an object for our love - an object that not only accepts our love but returns it as well. Because of the sexual nature of our bodies we fasten this affection on one person.

One of the great satisfactions of life is finding a mate and obtaining the great human expression of love through sexual union. When people have learned to love, and they know that love is divine and fills the whole universe and themselves, when they realize there is no fulfillment in life when love is denied, the world will see an end to failure of marriages.

"Keep love in your heart. A life without it is like a sunless garden when the flowers are dead."

–Oscar Wilde

When love is free to enter a person's world through their heart, it will pervade all the things they touch. Love will find perfect expression in their sex life with their mate, for we are all of the same nature and seek the same fulfillment, and shall find it through love, for love never fails.

The universe dances and sings, buds and blooms and builds. All of life clings one to the other and serves one another in a great common purpose. Love pervades all, love is behind all, and love is a great goal.

As a result your sex life, your relationship with your mate, expresses always your own understanding of love. But love never proceeds into the understanding solely through the relationship between mates.

The understanding of true love comes only from the relationship of a person with their spirit, of a person teamed up with the Universal Subconscious Mind, a person teamed up with God.

No human being can truly love another unless they first know the love of God. The Kingdom of Love is the Kingdom of Heaven, and exists within each man and woman.

A person who loves God loves life, loves themselves, and the nature of their lovingness will eternally come back to them. Their marriage will be a perfect fusion of their understanding of love, and all things of this world will shower them with goodness.

"Being deeply loved by someone gives you strength, while loving someone deeply gives you courage."

–Lao Tzu

Love creates, produces, heals, comforts, guides, and enlightens. Making yourself one with love is making yourself one with God, and God will work through you.

TRUST LOVE

We exist in a world which is striving to know and understand itself. Each of us is a miraculous manifestation of that world. There is a great and unknown spirit working in and through every person in this universe.

This spirit is seeking to know. We serve by living, loving and learning. By lifting our eyes to the stars, by asking questions, by searching for the answers. Life is the supreme adventure. We cannot fail if we keep our hearts filled with love and faith.

Trust love, for when you trust love you trust God. What is going on is a great and good thing, and we are a part of it. We shall always be a part of it. We do not need to be perfectly happy every minute of every day because perfect happiness only comes with perfect knowledge.

By trusting in the great and good ends of life and by knowing that the door to the mysteries swings on the hinges of love, we shall never lose faith in our divinity and our ability to build a heaven here on earth.

THE ADVENTURE OF LIFE

Through the desire for love, all things are created – our songs, our stories, our paintings, our engines and machines, our cities and schools, our churches and stores.

The hunger of mankind is to know the love of the great Creator. In all lands people are asking God to join with them in some enterprise. People are starting to realize that God doesn't join anybody – people join God.

God is love moving according to law. We must move over on God's side rather than ask him to move over on ours. God's side is the side of love. When we move toward love, we move toward God. We move toward peace, happiness, and knowledge.

Learning how to think and how to love, how to create through the use of Universal Mind are the main businesses of our lives. According to how we learn these laws all things come to us.

"The desire to create is one of the deepest yearnings of the human soul." –Dieter F. Uchtdorf

Every thought we think, every desire we have, every mood we invite, each motion we undergo, is projected into the great creative substance of the Universal Subconscious Mind to be manifested in the world about us. What a miracle! But also, what a responsibility.

According to how we think and what we believe it is done to us. Every minute of every day we are using the greatest power in the universe for good or for evil. God's will is love, and by following love as the guiding law of life, infinite power will be ours.

Every thought attracted by love and accepted by faith will create good in your world. There is no limit to love in the universe, and all of it is available to you.

Put this mighty medicine to work for you in your life, and you will see such a healing, a prospering, and peace that will dazzle your very eyes. Slowly the world is awakening to the truth.

CHAPTER 9: SUCCESS

Many of us have been fooled into thinking that successful people are the ones who make lots of money at other people's expense. In this chapter you will come to know the truth about success, how to obtain it, and how to make success your lifestyle. Andersen describes success as something on the inside of us and never something we have to fight, or even work hard for. Finding our passions through our service is key to obtaining success in all areas of our lives.

"Nothing in all the universe can stop our thoughts from becoming real in our experience, for that is the law of life and of living."

–U.S. Andersen

MONEY – A MEDIUM OF EXCHANGE

Success is a constant vision in the mind of modern man where we see ourselves surrounded by large homes, yachts, servants, trips, and people having plenty of time enjoying themselves.

"What obtains these things?" Asks modern man, and we answer quickly "Money." So we set off with this battle cry ringing, "Make money." It is little wonder that from this absurd false statement we scarcely are able to obtain enough to pay our bills.

The only people who "make" money are those employed in the various governmental minting houses; the rest of us earn it. We earn it by providing our fellow beings with services or products which are both needful and useful.

We go through our days exchanging our services for the services of our fellows and the exchange of money represents nothing more than the exchange of services.

Success is not the result of making money; making money is a result of success. It is always the fulfillment of the individual in productive effort that betters the welfare of mankind.

Modern man has got the cart before the horse. We set out to make money when in truth we should set out to be of service. Create! Build! Serve! Those are the commands of nature. Follow them and you will find there is no limit to the prosperity and abundance of the universe.

"The best way to find yourself is to lose yourself in the service of others."

–Mahatma Gandhi

Those who set out to simply make money, set out to accumulate money. Being interested in only acquiring money provides no service to mankind. Our moneymakers have defeated themselves from the start.

This is not to say that they may not, for some period of time, actually accumulate a certain amount of money; but they are certain not to be surrounded indefinitely with prosperity, for their premise is not to give but to get, and the law of the mutual exchange will catch up sooner or later.

Man has replaced hope, love and peace of mind with despair, hatred, and confusion by switching their worship from God to dollars. You cannot buy peace of mind.

MYTHS OF MATERIALISM

Abundance and prosperity are true spiritual conditions and are desirable and just for everyone. The pursuit of money for money itself is both senseless and degrading to the spirit, for it ignores the destiny of man. We are here to love people and use money. Not the opposite.

In America we have taught generations of children the myth of the "go-getter" and the legend of the millionaire. We have done each generation a great disservice.

The myth of the "go-getter" is rooted in the philosophy of dog-eat-dog" and millionaires are all too often the product of a greedy society. A person whose premise for success is founded on "taking away" is inevitably visiting upon themselves the same treatment.

THE YARDSTICK OF SUCCESS

Let money measure your service. Let your thoughts always be on the further service you can be to your fellows, and you will find their gratitude coming back to you in the form of money; perhaps not from the persons you have served, but return it will, for that is the law.

Take your satisfactions from service, constantly seek to expand and improve it. Take no thought for the money, which is always the results of service, and you will find yourself involved in an abundance that is unshakable for it comes from the roots of your soul.

"Everybody can be great… Because anybody can serve. You don't have to have a college degree to serve. You only need a heart full of grace. A soul generated by love."

–Martin Luther King Jr

Our success is measured always in the quality and quantity of service we render, and money is a yardstick for measuring this service.

Do not be tricked into believing people who have been enriched through swindles, violence and false promises. Nothing corrupt can stand. Prosperity based on falsehood is false prosperity and will wither away.

The lasting wealth of this world is rightfully won by those who have rendered service in equal measure. Such money is not "taken away" from anyone. It represents but a fraction of what has been created. The person who has surrounded themselves with a lasting prosperity has enriched the world through their efforts.

There is no limit to the abundance that can be created out of the limitless Universal Subconscious Mind and such abundance is available to all. No one can enrich themselves without enriching others, for the law of life is that we do not progress singly, but by groups.

Those who provide a great service cannot avoid a great reward any more than one who provides no service at all can avoid a condition of poverty.

POWER IS CREATIVENESS

Money then is never an end, never a means. Always it represents service only, for it is never more than a medium of exchange, and we can no more stop it coming our way when we are rendering service than we can start it coming our way when we are not rendering service.

Above all things, dispense the idea of "getting the best" of people. Each of us is like a pole in the flow of electric current. We absolutely cannot receive more current than we transmit and we always get back exactly what we send out. Moments in our lives, days, even months, we may seem to be giving more than we are receiving, or receiving more than we are giving.

But in the end the flow always balances. We never get the better of anything, nor are we ever dealt the worst. There are no bargains in living and no one is deceived except by themselves.

Mutual exchange is always with us; it is life itself. Those who recognize this will spend their hours developing their capacity to serve, build, create and give. No service you perform can possibly go unrewarded. No disservice can possibly go unpunished. The law of mutual exchange is the law of morality, of sin and punishment, of righteousness and reward.

How can we serve best? The answer is by creating and never by competing. We serve by creating new jobs, new markets, new means, and new methods. The magic that makes each of us what we are springs from an inexhaustible source. We are creative creatures tied to the creative power of God.

We create by our thoughts, miraculously, each moment of every day. Beneath the level of our consciousness there lies an infinite pool of knowledge upon which we may draw for every project we have the courage to embark upon.

Always "God gives threads to those who spin a web," and he smiles upon those who dare and aspire. No one is denied this creative power. It is the foundation, the root, the very essence of each of us. By working with it we are carried to dazzling heights. By opposing it we wither our lives in endless rounds of pointlessness.

"To accomplish great things, we must not only act, but also dream; not only plan, but also believe."

–Anatole France

UNMASKING THE EGO

Life is seeking to achieve. And always we achieve by creating. We achieve by seeking the center of consciousness, by becoming one with God and getting ourselves out of the way.

The thing we believe ourselves to be is never ourselves at all but merely a papier-mâché gown we have donned and pleased ourselves to call "I." This is ego, tricky, despoiling ego, a product of the awakening consciousness which is always attempting to isolate us and to separate us from our true being.

We wear a mask of vanity, this "I" of ours. Before we can truly learn to create, this mask must slip away. The ego must go. We must reduce ourselves so that we have eyes to see at last, eyes to see the towering dimensions of our true being. We must get our ego out of the way so the power can flow through.

Success depends upon service, and service depends upon achievement, and achievement depends upon creation, and all creation springs from Universal Subconscious Mind, which responds to us as we use it. How then shall we be creative?

We are, of course, all of us, already tied to the greatest creative power under the sun. We are using this creative power every moment of our lives. Indeed, we do little else than create.

Yet all too often we are using the power to bring unsatisfactory situations into our lives. More often than not we have become so mesmerized with fear and frustration that we reduce our existence to mockery. The question is not how we can be creative, but instead, how can we learn to create only good.

IMAGINATION AND CREATION

Universal Subconscious Mind protrudes through every conscious mind in the form of what we call imagination. This play of imagery has absolutely no limit upon it except that which we ourselves impose. All creative impulses spring imagination.

It matters not what your job is, whether you dig ditches or rule nations. The same power is available to anyone, and even the most exalted of the earth use but a tiny fraction of it.

If you will discard the false notion that security rests with material things, and place your faith and trust in the Universal Subconscious Mind, the power will go to work for you, creating in your life those very things which you allow yourself to imagine and except.

JOIN THE POWER

God seeks to know; through you he seeks an ever greater self-awareness. If you attune yourself with the expanding nature of life you will make yourself one with the purpose of God and success will surely come to you.

Success then, comes to you whose life is creative, and true creation brings forth into the material world the physical counterparts of thoughts, ideas, and conceptions aimed at the benefit of the human race.

Through opening the channels by which Universal Subconscious may operate through us, we arrange all things in our world. To be successful, we must think success.

To be surrounded by prosperity, we must think prosperity. The requirements is to put our great creative power to use through the love of God and the love of humanity. As a result we benefit others and life itself, and our good works return home to us in the form of success and prosperity.

"Look upon your desires – all of them – as the spoken words of God, and every word or desire a promise. Give thanks for it to the point that you are grateful for having already received it – then go about your way in peace."

–Neville Goddard

Nothing is done by man alone; all things are done by Universal Subconscious Mind in answer to thought and conception. What you think returns to you in physical reality, and when your thoughts are guided by love, good inevitably returns to you.

Turning your work over to God, letting love into your heart through perceiving the unity of all life, guarding the walls of the mind so as to think only positively – these are the elements of success.

THE SOURCE OF ALL IDEAS

Chance has nothing to do with directing great ideas to the people who have them. The idea finds its owner because the owner attracts it. We attract it by placing ourselves in a mental position where the idea must come to us.

We do this by removing from our mind all barriers as to what can or can't be done, all negative thoughts concerning limitation and lack, and we put our trust in the Universal Subconscious Mind, confident that it will deliver the answer.

Something better, greater, finer, more useful – those are the creative aims of all of us. The power is equally available to all, and it works in the life of each person according to their vision and understanding.

You need only to open your heart, become possessed by love, free yourself from racial thinking and pain remembrance, and the power will flow through. It will deliver to you anything you can ask for with faith and courage and clear conception.

Free yourself to ask the aspiring question, with complete confidence that the answer will come. Don't struggle with it. Don't doubt and wonder. Simply have confidence. In a day, a week, a month, the answer will come clearly as if a voice had spoken in your soul.

When the answer comes to your question, and a fine idea has been delivered into your life, you are a witness to the handiwork of God. If you are wise you will take a moment to regard this miracle with awe and humbleness.

Getting the idea simply involves opening your mind and heart to attract it, with complete trust that it will be delivered to you by Universal Subconscious Mind. Remain steadfast in your faith. The idea will come.

UNLOOSING THE FLOOD

Don't make the mistake of expecting that the idea will be delivered to you refined and tooled and ready for instant use. When the idea comes it will be general, and require patient examination and refinement.

Your purpose, then, must be to reduce the idea to its leanest, most beautiful, most useful form. Come to complete understanding of the aim of the idea and you will see the form take shape.

"If you have a worthwhile goal, find the one reason why you can achieve it rather than reasons why you can't."

–Napoleon Hill

The greater your faith, the clearer your image, the more readily it is impressed upon the Subconscious, and the sooner it will be returned to you in the physical world. If your idea was conceived in love, for service, for advancement, for creating, then abundance and success will be yours when it becomes manifest.

Do not rush about, hurry or worry. Your action will be guided by Universal Subconscious Mind, and all the things that you need for final success will be directed into your path, even as you are directed toward them.

"By day and by night I am prospered in all my ways."

–Joseph Murphy

Opportunity will eventually knock on your door, ring your telephone, greet you in the mail, visit you in the lunchroom, seek you at work and at play, so that you will wonder what flood has been unloosed. Those who work in tune with God have an unseen army aiding them.

The seed of success blossoms as well in any surrounding provided a person knows themselves and the power of Universal Subconscious. It is never the job that needs to be changed; it is the person holding it. We need to change our attitude, our mental outlook, to start thinking positively and creatively.

All of us, wherever we are, whatever our jobs, are sitting atop great opportunities to this very day. We need to get rid of denial, to open our hearts and our minds, to realize that the entire universe is moving forward at a great pace. We have only to hitch a ride and let the power carry us along.

THE HOBGOBLIN OF FAILURE

As with all things, prosperity and achievement are mental conditions. In order to achieve, you must first think achievement. In order to create you must first think creativity. In order to prosper you must first think prosperity.

Since few of us are in the situation we most desire, we have no alternative if we would achieve our goals, then to rise above our circumstances. We must not allow our thinking to be governed by the conditions around us. Our individual pain - remembrance prompters would have us believe that cause lies in the physical world. Then we become victims of circumstance instead of self-determining souls.

Do not be confused between the physical, which is always a result, and the mental, which is always a cause. Refuse to let circumstance grow into the image of your thought.

"We are all here for some special reason. Stop being a prisoner of your past. Become the architect of your future."

–Robin Sharma

The things that surround you, the circumstances that you are involved in, have sprung up from your subconscious desires. It will benefit you nothing to protest that this is not so. Facing this solid fact requires humility and very often considerable emotional suffering. But face it you must if you are to change your desires and change the world about you.

THE SEED AND THE HARVEST

Hard work is the fear of success for most of us. We see the immensity of our contemplated tasks even before we begin them. Imagination is both our blessing and our curse. Through it we perceive our aspiration, and through it is revealed the long road that sets us to despair.

Withdraw your mind from the seemingly impossible summit and turn your attention to the step to be taken today. Our steps through life are chains of cause and effect, and each step successfully taken delivers the next one to us with greater ease until in the end the final goal is ours.

"The way to get started is to quit talking and begin doing."

–Walt Disney

Today, this very day, is the most important time of all, for what we do today determines what we will be tomorrow. Therefore turn all your attention to your labors of the moment, absorb yourself, take your satisfactions from each thing you do, however humble in your own mind. Nothing is small or petty in this life.

MAKING HARD WORK EASY

There are no such things as hard work and easy work. There are only just distasteful work and enjoyable work. If you would make work easy, then enjoy it. Whatever you enjoy unlooses as a creative power that enables you to do it well.

A job well done leads to a greater job, and then still a greater, until your dream springs from mind to join you in the world.

Success comes to those who build their home with determined purpose, stone by stone, taking as great care with the first one as they do with the last, always knowing that the most important stone is the one they lay at the moment.

Hard work is made easy work through knowing that none of our labor is wasted. No matter the apparent thanklessness of your tasks, you can be assured that they are part of a purpose that will one day be fully revealed, a purpose grand and aspiring, which you become a part of when you keep the faith and persevere.

No task is too great for the one who leaves their plan in the hands of Universal Subconscious and concerns themselves solely with their day's work.

Inch by inch, foot by foot, step by step, is the kind of process life itself makes. Lasting success is evolved slowly, just as it requires a longer time to lay the foundations of a building that will tower the sky.

The satisfactions of the journey are always to be found on the way and never at the destination. If you have learned this you have learned peace of mind.

"Focus more on your desire than your doubt, and the dream will take care of itself. You may be surprised at how easily this happens. Your doubts are not as powerful as your desires, unless you make them so."

–Marcia Wieder

Let your work be an expression of love; as a result you will provide true service. All labor of love is not labor at all, but joyous self-fulfillment. Good works are simply love expressing itself, and a person whose heart is full of love does not need a pat on the back for their blood, sweat, and tears. Through this love of life we see in all work the opportunity to serve, and serve we do, and we fulfill ourselves and God.

THE RECKONING SCALES

The universe commands self-fulfillment and never self-sacrifice. Those who destroy their own life for some fancied thing, acts through vanity, and destroys a work that God has done.

Through each of us God has become a unique thing. By following the nature of our being to fulfillment we have satisfied the fondest commandment of life. It is no less evil to destroy ourselves than it is to destroy another.

The wise man will never sacrifice self, or their knowledge of self. All aims will be at ridding themselves of ego, at achieving unity with Universal Subconscious Mind, at communion with the center of consciousness. As a result success will come then prosperity. Success is a service, and money is a measure of it.

"Successful people are always looking for opportunities to help others. Unsuccessful people are always asking, "What's in it for me?"

–Brian Tracy

CHAPTER 10: HEALTH

Health of course is our most important asset in life. In chapter ten Andersen reveals the truth about health, how to heal ourselves, and how to help others. You will learn how we need only to surrender to health, except, and allow it. We need to trust in health completely and health will be ours.

"You have got to listen to the universe, to life, to God, whatever you want to call it. Because it is going to speak to you."

–Jillian Michaels

THE ORIGIN OF DISEASE

Health and well-being are the natural states of every form of life, for all things are rooted in Universal Subconscious Mind which is perfect. Physical health comes from mental peace, and disease and corruption comes from mental confusion.

So it is that man, the most intelligent of all forms of life, falls constant prey to disease and illness. Disease is a product of mental development. Those who have come to the full scale of self-consciousness but have not yet evolved the greater consciousness of immortal Self, sees themselves as an insignificant dot in a gigantic universe where they have not ordered their existence and cannot stay their death.

Our highly developed little ego cuts us off from the roots of our being, and we come to know fear, hate, and bitterness, all of which sets up conflicts between our emotions and our mind. These emotions projected into universal intelligence, cast our concept of ourselves from perfection and return to us as kidney stones, ulcers, high blood pressure, cancer, and so on.

Psychology and psychiatry have unmasked this chain of cause and effect so clearly that medical science, devised to treat disease as a physical thing only, now freely admits that 80% of all disease is of mental origin. It will not be much longer before this admission is enlarged to 100% where it should be.

A truth cannot be partly right, and it is obvious that all things have their origin in something greater than the physical world around us. Disease that is created is responding to something. That something is a thought or belief, formed by the conscious mind and projected into Universal Subconscious Mind, where it manifests in the physical world.

THE POWER THAT HEALS

It is a rare person who consciously desires to be sick, though it is certainly true that a few unhappy people have so completely cut themselves off from the spiritual unity of life that nothing further appeals to them than this form of slow suicide.

The vast majority of people fall prey to disease through negative thinking habits and through coping mechanisms established in answer to buried pain remembrances or prompters.

A person who is chronically ill has a subconscious desire to be sick, but to confront them with such a thesis would be to inspire the strongest denial. And even those of us who are sick only occasionally become so because it is a way of coping with situations that confront us.

Since we do not know ourselves or even who we are, we do not understand the dynamically creative energy in which we live, nor do we understand our subconscious desires, nor do we understand that each of these desires is delivered to us in reality.

So it is that all disease, all warping of the body from its natural physical perfection, comes because a person holds subconscious feelings of hate, bitterness, resentment, envy, jealousy, greed, self-pity, maliciousness, or any number of the countless unpleasant emotions that corrupt the natural expression of the universe – Love.

If a person does not love, they hate, for love is the power of the Universal Mind that flows to each person who lives, whether we use it positively or negatively. If we use it negatively, as in hate, it is a corrupting power and it weakens and decays and withers the body.

Once again we see that the commands of the universe are "Love or suffer." Love is the power that heals! Love banishes confusion, brings peace of mind, bands the door to negative thinking reveals the indwelling perfection of the human soul – The love for life and all its creations.

BODY IS ROOTED IN SPIRIT

Psychiatry is now only a skip and a jump away from being able to put its finger on the various negative emotions that bring on specific diseases. The day is not too far distant when medical textbooks shall list after hate, bitterness, frustration, repression, envy, and loneliness their result in physical debilities.

Mankind will guard its emotions with the same care it now offers to its physical well-being. Pills and potions will be replaced by healthy habits of thought.

"Your body hears everything your mind says."

–Naomi Judd

Our bodies are rooted in pure spirit, in Universal Subconscious Mind, which is perfect. Our bodies may be cast from perfection only by concepts held in the conscious mind, which project into Subconscious and are reported as physical ailments.

We did not cause our hearts to beat, nor do we direct the flow of blood to various organs, or the acids of the stomach to perform the miracle of digestion, or the intestines and kidneys to go about the process of eliminating waste. The dynamic source from which our bodies have sprung has instilled in them these reflexive actions.

The functions of the body represent the movement and concept of our intelligence, and when we get our fears and negative thoughts out of the way, our bodies function perfectly.

Every belief we hold of lack, limitation and despair performs its restricting influence on our bodies and in effect, the body does not function properly. As a result our self-awareness with its doubts and fears and frustrations limits the condition of our health and our lives.

We must let go of our little egos, take unto ourselves the God-consciousness which is our true being; then body becomes perfect, for we have become one with that which is perfect itself.

"Complaining is the absolute worst possible thing you could do for your health. I challenge you not to complain at all. What you focus on expands."

–T. Harv Eker

SPIRIT IS PERFECT

There is no such thing as an imperfect body, for body is always a perfect manifestation of an idea. There are only imperfect ideas. They are imperfect because they are in error, and they may be changed by simply accepting the idea of change.

A person who has suffocated their divinity in the belief that physical things are first cause is incapable of healing themselves until they have changed their belief.

If there joints are stiff and their digestion poor, they spend a good portion of each day acknowledging the fact that there joints are stiff and their digestion poor; and they themselves are thrusting their body into these very conditions by their belief.

They are deluded into believing that they think these things because of their ailments and cannot see that their ailments are because they think them so.

The intelligence that inhabits a person's body will become anything that is projected into it. It will make a healthy body if health is projected, and it will make a sick body if negative thoughts are projected. A healthy body is always the result of a healthy mind. If we were to heal our bodies, we must first heal our minds, with love, with recognition of our true being.

LET GO OF EGO

"A human being lives, moves, and has his being in a limitless ocean of health–power, and we use this power according to our faith."

–Wallace D. Wattles

Worry and tension, guilt and hostility, resentment and vanity lay the foundations for all of our physical afflictions. They spring like growths from our over developed little egos, which are forever being hurt and frustrated in a world which we set out to beat instead of cooperate with.

Victory seems to be all we can think of. We have to outshine someone, get the better of someone, make more money, be better looking or wear better clothes. How petty such victories are, and how unrewarding!

Find a champion and you will find behind them the shadow of the person who will replace them. There is no victory for the hounded little ego, for it is nothing by itself, and cannot see the larger dimensions of being in which it is rooted.

Turn to the gigantic self that dwells within and you will cease to be concerned with all the pains of your ego, which will immerse itself in an untroubled sea and bother you know more.

The entire miracle of existence and creation lies at your fingertips. Each day is a new birth, unlimited with miraculous possibilities for each person who lives.

FIND A MOTIVATING PURPOSE

Idea is a complete thing, aimed at purpose, and the body also a complete thing is aimed at purpose. It is this purpose which holds together the many interrelated functions of the body, and when purpose disappears from our lives our bodies start to disintegrate, even as the idea which manifested them is disintegrating.

A motivating purpose is absolutely essential to good health, for the organs and functions of the body respond to the goal in mind. When the goal is removed, sluggishness and irresponsibility overtake the body, and it decays and breaks down.

Nobody can be full and vigorous unless the mind that inhabits it is whole and vigorous, for the ideas we hold in mind are made visible through our bodies and the circumstances that surround us.

The first step to health is always the creation of interest and enthusiasm on the plane of mind. For the well-conditioned body is not a direct result of exercise but only a secondary result. True cause exists in the mind, as always, and a body is conditioned because of mental purpose, which causes purposeful exercise, which results in a strong body.

"It is not about perfect. It's about effort. And when you bring that effort every single day, that's where transformations happen. That's how change occurs."

–Jillian Michaels

EXERCISE AND HEALTH

Evidence shows that people of great purpose live to ripe old ages, so that it becomes an inescapable fact that interest, desire and aspiration are mental conditions that are always found in those who are healthy and strong.

Many sick people have been led back to strength and health simply by developing a consuming interest in a purpose. All things proceed from mind, which is always first cause. You need to start today by forgetting what's gone. Appreciate what you have, and look forward to what's coming next. Share your talents!

"Start each day by feeding your mind with mental protein, not mental candy. Imagine the feeling you'll have when you begin each day with a positive outlook, a hunger for success, and the confidence to make it happen."

–Brian Tracy

Physical strength is the result of strong thoughts, and physical weakness is the result of confusion. Therefore a person who accepts the perfection and power of the indwelling Self will find such perfection and power mirrored in their body. Health comes from within, and never from outside.

Our bodies are always perfect instruments of our thoughts, and perfect health may be ours whether we are athletes, professors, clerks, or housewives, if our thinking is clear with purpose and our hearts are free to love.

PAIN IS A SIGNPOST

The spiritual unrest of the world is evidenced by the increasing number of people over eating, over drinking, over-working, overplaying, and under-sleeping. We undertake such a chain of abnormal activity as an escape from the gnawing doubts, fears and frustrations that lie at the top of our subconscious.

Abuses of the body are always results of confusion in the mind. A subconscious sense of insecurity may lead a person into eating far too much, or a sense of being unloved may turn a person to alcohol.

We sometimes play too hard, seeking to forget the issues of life and death by burying our heads like ostriches. We often work too hard, seeking to amass a mountain of material gain to provide for our security, but we cannot take it with us when the transition comes.

We seek constantly for the pleasures of the senses, and by overindulging we dull the mystical creativeness of our true being. We learn slowly, mostly by pain, and each of our gains in knowledge and awareness is hard won.

Pain is that which visits us when we are in error, and through suffering we are turned back to the path of truth. Truly, we cannot be whole, either spiritually or physically, until we have recognized that the roots of our being rest in eternity.

Once we have come far enough to realize that all pain – physical, mental and emotional – proceeds from errors in thinking, we are well on the way to filling our lives with strength, abundance and joy; and have come a great step toward unity with Subconscious Mind.

DISEASE (DIS-EASE) IS NEVER INCURABLE

An infinite law is at work in the universe. It is the law of ideas becoming things. Since this law is the movement of Universal Mind, it has absolutely no limitation. Therefore there is no such thing as an incurable disease.

A law must work all the time in order to be law, and the law that governs the intelligence in which we are rooted is the foundation of all things.

Disease itself springs from an idea impregnated upon Universal Mind, and will be banished when the idea is banished.

"You can heal yourself! In fact you are the only one who can."

–Emmet Miller MD

Whatever disease science has been unable to find a cure for is not incurable. Something causes it; that something may be discovered and removed. Both medical science and psychiatry are learning that the root of all things exists in mind, springs from idea, and ideas can be changed.

Since there is no limit to idea and to the inexhaustible power of the Universal Mind, there absolutely cannot be any such thing as an incurable disease.

We must realize that the universe always turns out to be exactly what we think it to be, and so do our bodies. As we reach higher levels of consciousness, we take unto ourselves more perfect ideas, casting off the shackles of limitation, becoming aware that all things are possible.

The moment we say something is impossible, we make it impossible for God to manifest it through us. Another person with a greater vision and greater faith will bring it forth and they will allow God to work through them.

None of us have the right to say a thing is impossible, unless someone is foolish enough to place limitations on God. Perfect spirit is within us, willing to manifest perfect health for us if we but call upon it with faith.

MENTAL HEALING

Each person who suffers from ill health has usually fallen victim to a specific ailment. This specific ailment is the result of some obstruction in mind, some false idea, some erroneous conception.

When we heal the body by mental and spiritual treatment, we do not treat the body, we treat the mind. This is very important. One cannot get rid of result without first getting rid of cause.

Cause is always in the mind; bodily ailments are the result. All things spring from a perfect source, and we need only to contact this source and allow it to manifest its perfection through our bodies. So, the way to the healing of all disease is to recognize your spiritual perfection.

There is nothing in Universal Mind that desires our bodies to be warped away from the purposeful functioning for which they were intended. It is our conception of ourselves that visits disease upon us, and when we have conceived ourselves to be spiritually perfect, we become physically perfect.

The real you is not your body. Your body is but an extremely small extension in time and space. The real you is mental and spiritual, free of the confines of space and time, limitless in power and the capacity to understand and create.

When you have recognized your true spiritual self you have become identified with immortal Self, and disease cannot exist in your body, for there is no limitation in Universal Subconscious Mind.

TREATING FOR HEALTH

Disease is but limited thinking. We treat disease by refusing to accept it as having any true existence, by affirming the spiritual perfection in which we are rooted. Perfect love casts out fear, and perfect faith casts out physical imperfection.

We may call upon Universal Mind with the understanding that now is in us, and the Great Creator will respond by creating for us the image of our understanding. If we can find it in ourselves to allow spiritual perfection, Universal Mind will manifest this perfection in our bodies.

The process of spiritual and mental healing is affirmation. We waste no time dwelling on that which we do not desire. Our moments of consciousness are directed inward, at our spiritual selves, and are aimed at perceiving the perfection that gives us consciousness. What we see is returned to us. Awareness of the center of consciousness brings health.

AFFIRMATIONS:

-I am now allowing perfect health to flow throughout my body.

-Every cell in my body dances with the perfection of my Creator.

-I love my body and I'm allowing it to be strong.

"I give myself permission to be well."

–Louise Hay

"Every day in every way I AM getting better and better!"

–Bill Austin

"I myself, as much as anybody in the entire universe, deserve my love and affection."   –Buddha

-Ask Yourself: "Why am I so healthy?"

I AM LOVE

I AM WELLNESS

I AM PURE ENERGY

PERCEIVING TRUTH

Disease is a negative thought force, and therefor is illusion of the mind. In mental healing, we simply separate false thoughts from the true, consciously, and by allowing our faith and affirmations to sink down into our subconscious.

We admit physical strength and health into our lives. The principal of existence is the principal of thoughts becoming things. Since this is law, we do not argue or struggle with it.

RELY ON LAW

Mental treatment involves no personal responsibility other than for the idea and its affirmation. All else depends upon the principal of creation that underlies the universe; and this principal never fails.

When you affirm your spiritual perfection you are setting universal law in motion, which accepts your idea and the power of your affirmation, and manifests it in the physical world.

There is nothing superstitious about this. The law we are dealing with is infallible. It is true reality, beside which all else falls to nothingness.

Since disease (dis-ease) is caused by a mental condition, before it can be healed, the mental condition must be surrendered. A person, must first surrender themselves to God, the Universal Subconscious Mind. They must let go, give up struggle, trust in the invisible roots of their being, so that God-consciousness may engulf them and make them whole.

You cannot successfully treat yourself or another person until you are willing to surrender your doubts and fears, hates and hurts. The nagging emotional hurts we bottle up inside ourselves are like time bombs laid within. They explode in all the ills one human can develop.

We must surrender our fears, frustrations and guilts. Lay aside vanities and our little egos. Place all the hurts on the shoulder of the most high then we shall be free to partake of the beauty and perfection and abundance of the universe.

God is always right where we are, responding to us exactly as we acknowledge Him. The power for physical perfection is running over inside of us; we need only to surrender to it, accept it, trust ourselves completely to it, and health is ours.

When you treat yourself or someone for a physical ailment, remember that you are treating mind and not body. You are assuring yourself of mental and spiritual perfection. You are affirming, projecting it into Universal Mind with complete faith and trust.

When you treat someone else you still deal with the same mind. You treat yourself to think perfection of the person you are treating. Do not try to change the other person's thinking by the power of your own thoughts.

When you heal another you must be able to completely except in your own mind his or her spiritual perfection. When you have done that the healing will be effected.

"I open my heart to love and love flows through my every cell of my body, energizing, molding, coordinating strength."

–U.S. Andersen

CHAPTER 11: IMMORTALITY

Immortality is the ability to live forever, or eternal life. Andersen defines immortality as laying down one's body and moving into the great expansion where we become lord and master of all things.

We all seem to have our fears about death and the death of our loved ones. Without truly understanding death itself we create these fears that keep us in bondage in our daily lives.

Chapter eleven will bring understanding to the spiritual truths about our lives and where we are headed. As we take a look at our greater selves, death is but a graceful passing into the Kingdom of Heaven. A new and greater existence.

SPIRIT NEVER DIES

All too often those who search for the soul's immortality do so in answer to the question, "Will man live again?" and they cloud the issue, because if man be immortal man never dies; nor is man ever born, we simply "are."

That which has no ending can have no beginning, and that which has no beginning or ending is timeless and infinite, is pure being, and exists forever.

It is apparent that the body is not immortal. It has an obvious beginning and an obvious end. What we expect to be immortal in man is invisible, is spirit, a mysterious presence that brings the body to life with consciousness.

Each of us knows this presence very well, for it is what we feel ourselves to be. It is what we refer to when we say "I." This "I" then, this consciousness we know to be ourselves, is what we expect to continue on after the death of the body.

What and who is this "I"? Is it the accumulated memories of a lifetime? Is it the knowledge each of us has attained? Is it some central perception station at the nerve endings of the five senses?

Perhaps it is all of these, but it is a certainty that it is consciousness. That which is consciousness is capable of referring to itself as "I" and consciousness is invisible.

Consciousness is the sense of self that peers from behind your eyes and is the same sense of self that peers from behind the eyes of a friend or neighbor. Though this awareness is never at the same identical stage of development in any two beings, the difference is always one of degree and never of kind. Each of us is an expression of the immortal self. There is within us, the immortal self which was never born and will never die.

THE FALSE "I"

What is this deathless, ageless spirit that each of us sense in ourselves? How difficult to understand! Like mercury it slithers from under our finger tips the minute we try to grasp it.

For a moment we have a flash of insight, so that we seem right on the verge of discovering some mighty secret, then we begin to think about it and it disappears, leaving us wondering if we haven't imagined it.

Something blocks us away from the discovery. Some false habit of thought bars us from true knowledge of self. The culprit is the ego, the erroneous sense of self which we accumulate during our lifetime.

The death of the ego, which we fear so much, is the very thing we must achieve before we take unto ourselves the consciousness of immortal self.

"Ego closes your eyes for the truth.

Selflessness opens them.

Ego makes you lose your self-respect.

Selflessness gains it."

–Bhavesh Chhatbar

Let us reconsider the timeless, spaceless qualities of Universal Subconscious Mind, which has no beginning and no end. It is conscious but not self-conscious. Self without beginning or end incarnates and in doing so becomes something with a beginning. Anything with a beginning must have an end, and so the cycle of birth and death of physical bodies is established.

The accumulated experiences undergone by Self within the body gives rise to the feeling of separateness and isolation. This is ego. This is memory of the beginning of physical experience, and we are deluded into calling it "I."

In this manner we fail to perceive our true being and are shut away from the infinite and immortal intelligence from which we have sprung. Nearly everyone considers their ego to be their true self, and as a result is totally unable to comprehend a life after death.

REBIRTH OF CONSCIOUSNESS

Ego, the trapping of self-awareness bars us from consciousness of Universal Self. It perceives all things as existing outside of consciousness and deludes us into believing that all things originate on the physical plane.

It loads us with a sense of personal responsibility, causes bitterness and hate by its fancied wounds. It sees itself as a speck in a limitless universe and blows itself up all the bigger in a hopeless attempt to fill infinity. The question is not how shall the ego live, but how it shall die. For only when the ego dies do we truly begin to live.

The ego is mortal. It has its beginning and its end. When death overtakes the body, it also overtakes the ego. Freed at last from delusion, self knows self and sees its immortality.

The fear of death then, springs from the egos fear of death, but only because we cling to the ego as our true selves. Those who perceive at the center of consciousness the Great Self which is buried there will let go of the ego forever and move in tune with the infinite.

The death of the physical body frees us all from the bonds of the ego, but the unshackling of these bonds during our lifetime brings power. The death of ego is not a thing to be avoided, but a thing to be welcomed. A spiritual awakening that shines light on all things.

It is attained through humility, through love, non-resistance, through fusion with Universal Mind at the center of consciousness. Those who achieve this consciousness understands immortality.

One mind, one spirit, one Self pervades the universe, and its purpose is to know itself. Neither space nor time exists in it, for it is infinite. It is all form. It is becoming things. It becomes all things and each form it creates is an expression of its knowledge of itself. It is spirit. It is intelligence. It is mind. It is God.

Incarnating into form, it becomes that form, and when the form dissolves, the spirit again becomes universal. It is this in man which is immortal. Those who achieve awareness of the Self in life, achieve power.

Self is Universal Subconscious Mind, which is infinite. All of it exists within each of us. Infinity is absolute unity and cannot be divided. Therefore we must become aware of the timeless being that exists at the center of our consciousness. If we attain to this illumination or not, we are still immortal.

Everlasting life is not given to some and taken from others, for we are all one in reality.

FORSAKING THE EGO

Ego proceeds from the Conscious Mind, though they are not identical. Conscious Mind is the reception station at the nerve endings of the five senses. It is a classifying, analyzing machine.

It is governed by sensory stimuli and perceiving all things as existing outside of it. It builds habit patterns of work and a mass of experience and perceives the movement in time. As a result the ego is compounded of memory and prompts us to act always in the light of experience. According to the egos conception so our lives become.

This thing we falsely call "I," this ego, sees its limitations and brings those limitations into our lives. It fears, hates, and envies, for it seeks to constantly puff itself up by vain posture, by blind attitude, and it brings into our lives the physical result of these mental causes, and keeps us constantly in chains.

A person must first be meek and humble before they can become fused with immortal self. Sometimes people come to it through great suffering. Sometimes through great despair and pain, but always the ego is reduced to nothingness before the gate swings open.

The ego does not surrender lightly. This posturing little elf with its blind delusions would have us believe it is our own true self. When we attempt to cast it aside, we feel its struggles in the very depths of our souls.

So great is its resistance that men have mortified their flesh, practiced celibacy, abstained from all sensual pleasures in attempt to ignore the evidence of the senses so that the ego might leave and the center of consciousness revealed.

But there was never a need for such self-destructive practice. Quiet time with yourself for a few moments everyday can lead you to the results you desire.

THE AFTERLIFE

What will the afterlife be like? It will be like stepping from consciousness of a drop of water from the ocean into the consciousness of infinity. With the death of the physical body we shrug off the bonds of the conscious mind and ego.

We lay aside the limitations of flesh and become one with Universal Mind, pervading all time and places. We shall be in no specific place in the hereafter, for we shall be in all places. We will all be one, unified and indivisible, one Self, one mind, one eternal "I."

Life with its give and take, serve and be served, strive and accomplish, cannot in any manner be compared with existence in the hereafter. Life is the ego's day in the sun; the hereafter is the eternity of the Self.

"The Self cannot be pierced with weapons or burned with fire; water cannot wet it; nor can the wind dry it. It is everlasting and infinite, standing on the motionless foundation of eternity. The Self is unmanifested, beyond all thought, beyond all change. Knowing this you should not grieve."

–Bhagavad Gita

MOMENTS OF MYSTICAL EXPERIENCE

To everyone at some time in their lives have come to the startling magnitude of their own consciousness. Perhaps for a second only, and they have been overcome by question.

"Why do I live at this particular time, in this particular place, in these particular circumstances? What miracle has caused me to exist at all?" And at that very moment that person asking those questions stands very close to the veil, almost sees through it, almost understands what is beyond it, but not quite.

They are startled, a bit uncomfortable, seized by a strange sense of vertigo, wondering whether life itself is not a dream.

Usually we push aside this rare moment of mystical experience and concern ourselves again with the workday material world, taking assurance from the solidity of physical objects and the sharp definition of sensory perception.

And so we live like an ostrich, burring our heads in the sands of life, refusing to examine the most miraculous thing of all- our own consciousness. Where it has come from and where it is going.

Sprung from the everlasting Self into life, there is in each child the remembrance of Universal Mind. But as our ego develops, as we attain memory of sensory experience and the Conscious Mind grows, the memory becomes dimmer and dimmer, until we can recall it no longer, blocked from its view by the posturing ego which clutters the vision of spirit.

THE ANIMATING PRESENCE

That which is, was never born, and shall never die, is the very being of each of us. One Self, one mind. There is no difference between you and your neighbor except the ego of conscious mind.

The difference you perceive is the difference brought about through perception. Your neighbor is a product of every thought they have ever had, even as you are.

Since it is impossible for two reactive beings ever to have the same kind and sequence of thought, there has never been nor will there ever be two identical humans, short of union of God.

Everyone knows God exists, and not simply because we observe the other individuals responding to him. That which we feel ourselves to be we know as consciousness, lying within our body.

We observe other animated beings around us and correctly suppose them to be belonging to the same kind of consciousness as us; and we further observe death overtake the bodies of our loved ones, and note that the animating presence has departed.

We do not see where the presence has gone and we are mystified. We further observe that this condition of death, or departure is inevitable to all forms of life and inevitable to us, so we vainly try to peer beyond that event in order to determine if we might exist after our bodies have ceased to function.

Finally, after struggling with these thoughts, the question becomes too great for us because we cannot imagine an existence without our bodies. We end up throwing up our hands in despair and decide that our consciousness resulted from the fantastic army of circumstance that produced our bodies and that on either side of birth and the grave there is nothing.

But none of us completely accept this delusion. No matter how vociferously we may proclaim it. There is something in us that knows differently. That something is Self, the presence that animates our bodies. Birthless, deathless, and ageless, it knows about living forever.

SELF IS NOT BODY

Your body is not you. If it were and your leg was amputated, part of your consciousness would be lost with your leg. Neither are you simply brain. If you were only brain, then the rest of the physical body could be stripped away, and the brain would continue to live.

Actually, the brain itself does not even think. Some invisible thinker merely uses the brain as a central reception station for sensory perception.

Someone, something is dwelling in your body, peering through the windows of your eyes, listening at the portals of your ears, using your brain to receive impressions.

"The moment I have realized God sitting in the temple of every human body, the moment I stand in reverence before every human being and see God in them–That moment I am free from bondage, everything that binds vanishes, and I am free."

–Swami Vivekananda

It is invisible, hidden, gowned with your particular form, then departs to the source from which it came. People want to know where they go when they die. The answer to that question is that they do not truly go. They simply expand.

Self, freed from limitations of body, becomes Universal Self, the consciousness of all time, space, and form. When Self is free of all limitation, it leaves behind personality, ego, and conscious memory, which becomes immersed like the tiniest drop of water in an infinite sea. Ego goes, limitation goes. The inconceivably small "I" is replaced by the great "I" of infinity.

BEHIND EVERY PAIR OF EYES

It is always the ego that blocks "living forever" from view, for the ego cannot see beyond its own limits. It needs a body and separateness, for from these conditions it has sprung, and it projects a hereafter that revolves around bodies and personalities.

Body, personality, and Conscious Mind change throughout life. How shall they exist then in the hereafter of the ego? They all have no further use when we return to the infinite.

The great Self enters into each body and becomes different according to what enters, but upon leaving again becomes absolute unity.

NO PUNISHMENT IN THE HEREAFTER

It is one of the strangest facts of history that the words of the Bible have been misconstrued to saddle mankind with a vengeful God who bargains with the devil for souls.

Immortality is not something to be won by good conduct, nor will good conduct send certain souls to heaven, nor bad conduct to hell. Only one Self manifests throughout the universe, and it neither punishes or rewards itself.

It is eternal, and through it becomes a billion living things. Its eternity is not touched. Obviously it neither sends itself to heaven or hell, for nothing exists outside itself.

Have no fear of hell – there is no such thing. There is only heaven, which each of us shall eventually attain, whether it comes to us in life as we make it so or not.

"Earth is crammed with heaven…But only he who sees, takes off his shoes."

–Elizabeth Browning

EVERY SOUL IS SAVED

Misapprehensions concerning sin, punishment, hell, and the devil come from lack of understanding of the message of God. The truth about each person lies in their spirit and not in the physical world.

"Seek not greatness, but seek truth and you will find both."

–Horace Mann

Sins refer to errors of thinking, buried guilts and punishment is the inevitable physical manifestation of such negative thinking. By hell is meant the human bondage undergone by each person who simply reacts to the physical world and fails to perceive their inner consciousness.

Awaken to your spiritual power; turn your eyes from the physical world onto the consciousness that lies within so that you may free yourself from lack, limitation, and disease.

We must come to realize that God is kind, just, loving, and is in us. There is no punishment in the hereafter, and every soul is saved. We do not need to fear God; we need only to love Him. We do not have to beg for forgiveness before an alter, for God's alter is our very selves. We are him night and day.

Religions and temples are built by man, but God's temple is man, and wherever we are. We only need to turn to the Self that dwells within.

THE ART OF DYING

Birth and death are the great transformations. The ego does not fear birth for there is no ego at birth. The ego indeed fears death. As long as we identify ourselves with ego, the fear of death shall have its hold on us, and we shall regard it as a great distress.

Once we have freed ourselves of the ego and have perceived at the center of consciousness the immortal self, death will become an adventure. By it we shall be freed from illusion, return to absolute truth, and become united with God.

Life is the medium through which the great Self seeks to work out its purpose, and each of us as a part of that purpose has our appointed tasks and work. When these are fulfilled it is time for us to return home once again.

Many people poison their lives through fear of death. Since death is known to be inevitable for everyone, it is indeed very strange that so little is known in the art of dying.

"The day which we fear as our last is but the birthday of eternity."

–Lucius Seneca

To most people death comes when the body is worn out and ceases to function, and is preceded by a period of time in which the body begins to break down.

As the hour of death approaches, the human soul has only two ways to turn; outward for the comfort of the physical world or inward to the universal Self.

A painful death awaits those who turn to the outer world, for they are prompted by the ego which seeks to hold on to that which must be let go. Those who identify themselves with ego undergo a confused and suffering transformation.

But those who have viewed the greater Self takes death calmly. Assured of immortality and the changlessness of spirit, they pass easily from one world to another. Their spirit lays down their body because it is finished with it, and moves into the great expansion where it becomes lord and master over all things.

Self meets self, the personal becomes the universal, and a new and greater existence in the infinite reduces the just finished life to nothingness, to a second in the endless time of eternity.

And so we die as we have lived, with or without faith. With spiritual knowledge or without. According to wisdom we have attained, we meet death gracefully or crudely, but each of us is immortal nonetheless.

"Our creator would never have made such lovely days, and have given us the deep hearts to enjoy them, above and beyond all thought, unless we were meant to be immortal."

–Nathaniel Hawthorne

There is an answer to every question, a solution to every mystery, a key for every lock. Throughout this book we have prepared you for the final revelation. Now it is upon us.

CHAPTER 12: THE KEY

THE VEIL REMOVED

This is the extreme secret, the ultimate illumination, the key to peace and power: You are God.

If you will accept this towering truth, dare to stand atop this magnificent pinnacle, universal consciousness will be revealed to you.

God is there. It is He who peers from behind your eyes, who is your own consciousness, who is your very Self. You are not just a part of God; you are altogether God, and God is altogether you.

"We have seen that when we examine the World's major religions, we find within them without exception the idea that a person's real identity is God. The ultimate truth has always been for most people the unbelievable truth."

–Wai H. Tsang

God is Universal Subconscious Mind, the intelligence that pervades all times and places. The design, order and consciousness of all things. He has become YOU.

God is not your body, not your ego, but your sense of being, your "I" in the universe. The same sense of Self is in everyone. It appears to be different in life because it clothes itself in different forms.

These forms wither and decay, but the Self is always one and indivisible and changeless. Every person that lives, every person that will ever live, every creature and thing are all one spirit.

Each of us is altogether God because infinite intelligence cannot divide itself. It makes a seeming division in flesh, but never in spirit. God manifests completely in each thing, and each thing is a manifestation of God's knowledge of Himself.

Your consciousness is God's consciousness. Your idea of yourself is God's idea of Himself. The ideas you accept are automatically manifested in life, for what God knows He creates, and what you know is created, for you are God.

UNIVERSAL CONSCIOUSNESS

God is consciousness, awareness, order, design, knowledge, intelligence, and spirit. He is infinite but cannot know himself as infinity, but only by becoming things.

What you believe yourself to be is what you believe God to be. The limitations and lacks you impose upon yourself you impose on God. No one can possibly believe there is any limitation on God, as a result there is no limitation on man.

Through each of us God attains self-consciousness, and each of us is God incarnate. In our lives we accept the limitations of the flesh and the inhibitions of the ego, and we fall short of God-consciousness.

We ask ourselves where we have come from and where we are going, for we have lost the remembrance of having always been, just as we cannot see that we will always be.

"How can God possibly be the poor thing that I am?" a person will ask themselves, identifying themselves with ego and failing to perceive that they are consciousness only. Free yourself from the bonds of the ego, and you will forget the poor thing that you thought you were, and become one with God.

ILLUMINATION

This far you can be guided but the attainment of enlightenment is yours to achieve alone. Words and logic have never yet provided the great illumination, which must come to each person in their own way.

If you will accept with perfect faith the premise that all truth is spiritual, if you will discard the promptings of the ego and noisy sensual stimuli of the material world, if you will search for revelation at the center of consciousness, then the Kingdom of Heaven will be yours. Letting go of ego may seem like letting go of life itself, and so it is.

FIND THOU BUT THYSELF

Though this knowledge is not new, it has been exceedingly rare and held among the few. All the ages of life's evolution, up through the slime and mist of a newly formed earth have pointed toward it.

"A person's real identity is God. This would not seem obvious to most people and the reason for this is that this most ultimate of truths is usually kept hidden from the masses and only revealed to a chosen few who are initiated into these higher mysteries. This truth has historically found itself censored and suppressed."

–Wai H. Tsang

There is only one consciousness in all things, one consciousness which assumes countless forms in search of ever greater knowledge of itself. The infinite Self becomes the finite self, and the day when finite self recognizes itself as infinite Self is the day that exposes eternity.

This little hour, this little life where we are focused now, is but an instant in the eons of our being. We are that very power that constructed the heavens and the earth, and when we have cast out ego and the limitations of our thinking, the multi-dimensioned heavens are revealed to be in our own souls.

We have looked in the mountains and He has not been there. We have looked on the plain and He has not been there. We have searched the sea, the air, earth, and sky, and He has not been there. How should we find Him when we looked outside? He dwelt within, was in our very selves the whole time.

LOCK AND KEY

The lock that bars us from the recognition that we are God is the creation of the ego in the first memories and inhibitions of the Conscious Mind.

This lock may be undone through meditation, through taking unto ourselves universal consciousness; and the key that unlooses all power is the revelation that each and every one of us is God.

When our consciousness expands beyond ego, beyond conscious mind, beyond the limitations of the negative prompters, thoughts are immediately manifested on the physical plane.

Thought transference, clairvoyance, mental healing, and creativeness are all evidences of the super-physical power of Universal Subconscious Mind.

We add all things unto ourselves by taking a position with impregnable faith. Faith moves Universal Mind to creation, but it is only the ego that must use faith.

When the ego goes the God-consciousness comes. Thought is immediately followed by the thing, for there remains nothing to overcome. Whatever God knows is created.

We attract into our lives the physical manifestations of the thoughts we think, and in order to attract good instead of evil we must learn to control our thinking, to think positively instead of negatively.

"In the instant of our first breath, we are infused with the single greatest force in the universe–the power to translate the possibilities of our minds into the reality of our world. To fully awaken to our power, however, requires a subtle change in the way we think of ourselves in life, a shift in belief."

–Greg Braden

When a person thinks only in response to a stimuli of the outer world they remain only ego, an automation. But when we originate thoughts at the center of consciousness, we create our own lives in the image of our own desires.

"'Freedom' is but another word for 'God.' It has been difficult to find words in the human language to describe that which is God, but 'Freedom' is one of them. Another word to describe God is…YOU."

"You and God are One. Therefore you, too, are Free. Free to make choices, free to select your reactions and responses to life, free to be your authentic Self."

–Neale Donald Walsch

Before I leave you with all of this beautiful insight I'd like to share one of mine…

We have all been hurt by people we love or have loved. For me, experiencing that in my younger years had caused me to feel that God was untrustworthy. I was always comparing the two! I finally realized that by doing this, it was causing a great barrier between me, God and the life I desired! We as a whole are and have been working toward our Divinity and people will make mistakes. God on the other hand already and always has been The Divine (supremely good) and the one to trust wholeheartedly. When I realized this my faith was restored 100% and I no longer compared the two.

Once you start seeing God as the "Loving Deliverer" of your desires and your Best Friend who wants nothing more than to make you happy, you will no longer struggle with the feelings of discontentment, and your faith will be restored. You will start to see your desires come into fruition and smile on how easy they come to you. As you dream, use your imagination, and feel those things that you wish to be a part of your reality as already given, you will see the manifestation of them happening right before your eyes. Sending out feelings of gratitude for the things that are coming your way will allow them to speed toward you more quickly.

You and God are ONE, and nothing in this world can separate the two of you. It's time for you to except these truths and start allowing the life you desire. You deserve nothing but the best this life has to offer... and yes this means <u>YOU</u>!

I believe you are Awakened.
You are Divine.

Thank You Uell Andersen for Being That Bright Light in Our World.

With Lots of Love,
Tricia Topping

Made in the USA
Lexington, KY
05 May 2015